GODISNOWHERE

where is God in the midst of your pain?

mickeystonier

A LAMP POST BOOK

WHAT PEOPLE ARE SAYING ABOUT GODISNOWHERE

"At a time when our world is struggling to come to terms with the craziness that surrounds us, Mickey's book is both timely and instructional. I forever will be in his debt for the service he has provided to San Diego's fire fighters."

Jeff Bowman, Fire Chief, Orange County Fire Authority

"Mickey Stonier is uniquely qualified to write this book, with his many years of pastoral and chaplaincy ministry experience. He has seen it all and walked beside those facing life's greatest challenges. *GODISNOWHERE* is full of spiritual insights, Godly wisdom, and sage counsel (and quite a few reality checks). You'll be encouraged and challenged as you read it."

Mark L. Strauss, Ph.D., University Professor of New Testament
Bethel Seminary San Diego

"Having responded to disasters and crisis situations around the world, I have seen both questions and accusations arise from the survivor, 'Why God?' *GODISNOWHERE* dives deep into the complexities of this universal cry and gives the tools to assist the suffering."

Sean Malone, Founder of Crisis Response International

"This book sets the Gold standard for all things ministerial. From Ground Zero at 9/11 to the most mundane human problems, Dr. Mickey Stonier has the experience, Bible knowledge, and spiritual insight to show that God is way to overcome adversity—be it human or supernatural."

Bob Freiberg, United States Navy Chaplain (Ret.)

"Our world is rapidly changing and current events cry out for a need of HOPE in the midst of growing chaos. *GODISNOWHERE* is a very timely source of practical insight and spiritual support for those needing help navigating through life's injustices and hardships."

Tom Phillips Billy Graham Evangelistic Association Vice President, BGEA
Executive Director Billy Graham Library

"Trauma and loss are common human experiences. Unfortunately, first responders get a front row seat to it over and over again. Mickey Stonier's experience and wisdom shine through in *GODISNOWHERE*. This is a must read for those who have been there, and those who will experience tragedy and loss."

Chief John Bolduc, San Diego Harbor Police

"Dr. Stonier has skillfully written a practical and compassionate guide through God's plan for healing the damage created by the harshness of life. When the storms batter us, it is common to find ourselves confused, angry, and hopeless. This book offers the reader an opportunity to re-calibrate their heading and set a course for renewal and peace."

Charles A. Owens, Th.D., LCDR, United States Navy Chaplain Corps

"An amazing book that will help navigate its readers through the chaotic nature of society today and provide practical examples of how leveraging one's faith will overcome life's most formidable challenges no matter how unfair things may seem. *GODISNOWHERE* is ideal for those who have suffered personal set backs or traumatic losses, like my wife and I experienced when our 16-year-old daughter was killed in an accident. It is perfect for Bible study, personal enrichment, and for married couples to grow together in their walk with the Lord."

William D. French, Vice Admiral United States Navy (Ret.)

"This book is a blessing! I've known and respected Rev. Stonier for over two decades. *GODISNOWHERE* is a truly unique and valuable contribution to the field of pastoral crisis intervention. This must-read book integrates scripture with the science of crisis intervention. No other book that I have read does so in such a practical, yet credible manner."

George S. Everly, Jr., PhD, ABPP, FAPM, FAPA
Associate Professor of Psychiatry and Behavioral Sciences
The Johns Hopkins School of Medicine and ICISF NGO Delegate to the United Nations

"Mickey Stonier has been a good friend for more than twenty-five years and I have had the privilege of seeing him come alongside thousands of hurting people with a combination of divine compassion and rock-solid truth that actually makes a difference. There is no one I would rather have by my side during a crisis than Mickey. *GODISNOWHERE* provides real hope and practical help for anyone going through a painful experience. Each chapter is packed with real, life-tested principles and practices that will help you experience the goodness of God in the midst of your greatest challenges. This is a must read for anyone in crisis!"

George Clerie, church planter, Founder of Impact195,
Executive Pastor of Global Ministries Rock Church

"To presume we may avoid the burden of pain, injustice, or suffering is naïve at best, and arrogant at worst. It is through this journey of pain that the grace and mercy of God becomes most evident. Mickey Stonier is calling forth from each of us the passionate need to embrace the pain and allow God to be with us in forming wholeness through it. In practical and Scriptural ways, he invites our hearts to see in the midst of suffering that God's present presence is our healing. God is Now Here!"

Rev. Kevin W. Mannoia, Ph.D. Chaplain &
Professor of Ministry, Azusa Pacific University

"Dr. Stonier advocates a trialogue uniting theology (God perspective), the social sciences (human perspective) and 'relational encouragement' for a Christian Worldview, which addresses the posed problem and solution of human suffering and social injustice, rooted in a Biblically-based theology and practical methodology."

Earl E. Grant, PhD, DMIN, ThM, MDiv, MA, Four Year Visiting Scholar for the
Oxford Centre for Mission Studies, Oxford University, Senior Professor Emeritus,
Comparative and Practical Theologian,Azusa Pacific Seminary

"Best book ever. Just shut up and read it. Forget about it!"

Tony DiGiacomo, Italian New Yorker, friend

GODISNOWHERE

by Mickey Stonier

Trade Paperback: ISBN-13 # 978-1-60039-234-4
ebook: ISBN-13 # 978-1-60039-741-7

Library of Congress Control Number: 2016951145

LAMP POST inc.
www.lamppostpublishers.com
Spring Valley, CA

To my amazing wife, Karen,
proof that in marriage
God saves the best for last.

Contents

Acknowledgments

As a young pastor I was fortunate to have a number of years with the wise input from Dr. Sherwood Eliot Wirt. Woody, as his friends called him, was the founding editor of *Decision Magazine,* author of forty-two books and a long-time associate of Billy Graham. As an encouragement, Woody gave his sage advice to us younger ministers to wait until we were sixty-years old before writing a book. He affirmed that the twenties and thirties are a season for learning and laying a strong foundation for one's life and ministry. Woody taught that the forties and fifties would be the most fruitful years of accomplishment and achievement. He then jested to me that I probably shouldn't write a book until I was sixty because anything I'd write before then, would most likely need to be re-edited with the wisdom that comes with age. Truly this has been wise advice, especially when dealing with the subjects of God's providence, human suffering, and divine redemption. Yet, I am pretty confident that I'll continue to reflect and adjust my thinking on the subjects in this book until everything becomes crystal clear when I see God face-to-face.

Growing up with a father who was a police officer and two older brothers, John and Pat, who assisted their communities as public servants and emergency responders, it was modeled for me that there is no greater love than to lay down one's life for others. Also serving in relationship with so many chaplains and pastoral care team members at the Rock Church, I am constantly reminded of our commission to bring pervasive hope to every street and every person, no matter what the situation may be. In an era of racial and political tension, I am so blessed to be a small part of a diverse team of servants who simply want to make God known through our love for one another and our love for those in need.

As a result of over six decades of learning, there have been many professors, mentors, friends, and family members who have invested into my life that gave birth to *GODISNOWHERE.* In addition, I am overwhelmed by the love of a close family that demonstrates to me the kindness and grace of God on a daily basis, and reminds me that to whom much is given, of them is much required. I want give special thanks to my pastoral friends and mentors, Miles McPherson and Mike MacIntosh, for their years of ministry guidance, integrity, and passion to serve God's people in the grace of the Gospel. In addition, I need to express my appreciation for my good friend and professor,

Dr. Earl Grant, who taught me the balance of laughter and levity when pressing further into scholarship and higher education.

Of course this work would not be as respectable as a finished manuscript without the guidance, counsel, and editing work of Brett Burner, Wayne Kinde, Lynn Vincent, Madalene Stonier, Julia and Matt Redlitz, Shiloh and Preston Caffrey, Michael and Alexis Stoniea, Chuck Allers, and Carmen Munnelly. And finally, I want to acknowledge George Clerie, Joe Davis, John White, Jerry Paradise, Charlie Owens, Bob Freiberg, Garrett Graupner, Shawn Wagner, and Lee Shaw who have taught me so much about the proper care of people who are growing through horrific seasons of brokenness and loss. I am blessed to be a part of a rich community overflowing with love, laughter, grace, compassion, and humility as we do life together while on mission to bring healing to a fragmented world.

Introduction

Trauma is often sudden, unexpected, and overwhelming. Life is swung out of balance and there is a numbing sense of shock and disbelief. Other times the suffering is a long drawn-out process over months, or even years. It can be natural to doubt and question one's core beliefs and assumptions about the nature of reality and its governing principles.

Within the cryptic phrase "GODISNOWHERE," we find two polarized conclusions that align well with people's responses to a calamity. During a crisis, some will reject their faith as they cry out, "God is *nowhere*!" Others, though, experience a faith transformation and assert, "God is *now here!*" These variant responses within the human heart become a marker in discerning the true nature of one's soul. When our circumstances appear to dictate that we have been abandoned by God, His promises hold true that, even in the most painful of times, He is present and intimately at work to bring us hope and comfort.

It is within God's secret mysteries of grace that we must venture to come face to face with our mortal musings of self-exaltation and live within Romans 8:28, even when it hurts or appears senseless: "And we know that all things work together for good to those who love God, to those who are the called according to His purpose."

Yes, the eternal God has secrets. And sometimes God doesn't tell. "The secret things belong to the Lord our God, but the things that are revealed belong to us and to our children forever, that we may do all the words of this law."[1] Yet at other times, He does tell. Why?

Perhaps this is the wrong question to ask…

When life hits us on the side of the head, it isn't *why* or *how* or *when* or *what* that should define our quandary, but instead, *Who!* God doesn't always give us explanations; rather God gives us His promises. When the circumstances of one's existence seem to totter on the insane, the Lord can quiet the soul and temper one's anxieties as He shouts His ever-present help in our trouble.[2] C.S. Lewis' assertion has echoed through a great many writers on this subject: "Pain insists upon being attended to. God whispers to us in our pleasures, speaks in our consciences, but shouts in our pains. It is

God doesn't always give us explanations; rather God gives us His promises.

1 Deuteronomy 29:29 ESV.
2 Psalm 46:1.

His megaphone to rouse a deaf world."[3] When a child skins his knee after a stumble, it is not the safety lecture that will alleviate his "owie;" instead the tears evaporate within the embrace of a parent's reassuring presence.

When we are falsely accused, Jesus whispers to us, "I will never leave you nor forsake you."[4] Should we ever hear the harsh rejection, "you're fired," God's megaphone resounds with, "'Do not be afraid of them, for I am with you and will rescue you,' declares the LORD."[5] When at the hospital waiting for results, He affirms, "Only be strong and of good courage."[6] In the midst of a sudden crisis when your heart is completely overwhelmed, God can lead you to the Rock with a better vantage point.[7] At those times when no words can put into perspective the anguish you are feeling, God promises, "I will uphold you with My righteous right hand."[8] And right around the corner we are reminded that His hand spans the heavens.[9] It is in our moments of deepest despair that the living God resuscitates us to our living hope.

> "Blessed be the God and Father of our Lord Jesus Christ, who according to His abundant mercy has begotten us again to a living hope through the resurrection of Jesus Christ from the dead, to an

---

3 Lewis, C.S. (1944). *The Problem of Pain.* The MacMillan Company, New York, NY, p. 93.
4 Hebrews 13:5 (NKJV).
5 Jeremiah 1:8 (NIV).
6 Joshua 1:6, 7, 9 (NKJV).
7 Psalm 61:2.
8 Isaiah 41:10 (NIV).
9 Isaiah 48:13.

> inheritance incorruptible and undefiled and that does not fade away, reserved in heaven for you, who are kept by the power of God through faith for salvation ready to be revealed in the last time."[10]

The crucible of suffering is renowned for producing some of the chief virtues within human nature. Even our most precious treasures of gold, diamonds and pearls share this common refinement—through the conditions of heat, pressure and irritation. I have discovered great value in my own transformation within God's amazing grace through the faith-disciplines of prayer, study, solitude, fasting, service and worship. And yet, without diminishing these essential mercies, I believe there are equally four sharp tools that the Master Potter uses to mold, shape and fashion His character in us that are seldom mentioned as means of God's grace. In fact, when on the Potter's wheel, I have found these four implements perhaps most effective in cutting away at my deep-rooted self-promoting warts: (1) Times of suffering, (2) Times of failure (3) Dealing with injustice and false accusations, and of course the most heart-wrenching of the four, (4) Times of being a witness to the suffering of those we love the most. It is during these experiences when we are hurt most deeply that we find God intentionally working to reform us most purely.

These are the seasons in life when one's heart will bargain with God freely to release our dearest idols that are otherwise excused as acceptable within times of serenity.

10 1 Peter 1:3-5 (NKJV).

Our anguish tempts us to self-focus and whimper to God, "Why me?" But perhaps the greater question within the promise of potential soul-transformation during hardship should be, "Why not me?" A devotional reflection by L.B. Cowan that has encouraged my heart affirms:

> "The best things of life come out of wounding. Wheat is crushed before it becomes bread. Incense must be cast upon the fire before its odors are set free. The ground must be broken with the sharp plough before it is ready to receive the seed. It is the broken heart that pleases God. The sweetest joys in life are the fruits of sorrow. Human nature seems to need suffering to fit it for being a blessing to the world."[11]

This lesson was taught anew to my wife and me when we were called upon to comfort our dear friends who were in pastoral ministry during an occasion of extreme loss. Their twenty-two-year-old daughter, who struggled with mental illness since adolescence, had been on suicide watch. During the commotion of a busy family evening, the parents justly panicked when their daughter didn't respond to their calls throughout the house. A frantic search found their daughter a victim of suicide in their backyard. This phone call, with the piercing cries at the other end, will linger in my memory as one of those reverberating echoes that last a lifetime. However, it wasn't until my wife and I sat

11 Cowman, L.B. (1925). *Streams in the Desert: Volume 1.* Zondervan Publishing, Grand Rapids, MI. p. 255.

on the floor of their hotel room, wailing together with this couple, that Jesus' comfort and presence exceeded human capacity to comprehend. As the parents narrated the experience of the preceding night over and over hoping to erase reality, a quiet came into our presence. It was as if the air was sucked out of the room. And in one of the most profound moments of divine revelation I have ever experienced, the father expressed that he believed he was tasting of a morsel of the eternal love that his heavenly Father had displayed for us all. Breaking through the tears, this dad identified greatly with what God had endured for our sins by sacrificing His one and only Son, Jesus Christ, on the cross at Calvary. God had done this for us, not while we were in our most lovable state, but rather, while we were most despicable, Christ died for us.[12] It is nearly impossible to express with words the extraordinary insight that this father had while in the midst of his anguish. As tears revived with a greater force, I was witness to the tears of grief turning into tears of intense love at the sacredness of the cross, which in turn illuminated such a dark night.

Over the years, I have observed that for a pastor to grow in having the heart of God for the care of the church, the minister often studies much, prays much and suffers much. It is this refinement by the Holy Spirit that can produce some of the most precious work in us. When our flesh is crucified, Christ is manifested more clearly.[13] In the brief year that followed for my friends, I was witness to a couple who humbly reflected the love of Christ to others

12 Romans 5:8, 8:32.

13 cf. Galatians 2:20.

with a depth of grace and compassion unique to those who have been carried in the arms of the Chief Shepherd. Paul the Apostle testifies of a similar heart and life course when the Lord penned through him,

> "Blessed *be* the God and Father of our Lord Jesus Christ, the Father of mercies and God of all comfort, who comforts us in all our tribulation, that we may be able to comfort those who are in any trouble, with the comfort with which we ourselves are comforted by God. For as the sufferings of Christ abound in us, so our consolation also abounds through Christ. Now if we are afflicted, *it is* for your consolation and salvation, which is effective for enduring the same sufferings which we also suffer. Or if we are comforted, it is for your consolation and salvation. And our hope for you *is* steadfast, because we know that as you are partakers of the sufferings, so also you will partake of the consolation."[14]

Oh, and did I forget to mention that the pastor's wife's mother was murdered, and her father died of Alzheimer's disease shortly after her daughter's death, and her husband (and pastor) died of a stroke a year after their daughter's suicide? There are no explanations that I can conjure to fix the depth of pain that some people experience, but nevertheless, God's promises hold true to the core of His eternal

14 2 Corinthians 1:3-7 (ESV).

nature of love. I know this to be true as I see Christ's reflection in our friend who continues to joyfully serve the Lord on staff at a church in her new community.

Theologians have a unique term to describe the dilemma of human suffering in the acknowledgment of an all-powerful, gracious God. If the God of love is completely good and incomparably powerful, why does suffering exist? It is at the base of this philosophical monolith that the concept of "theodicy" was birthed. Theodicy is derived from the two root words, *theos,* "God" and, *dike,* "justice." The German philosopher Gottfried Leibniz (1646-1716) originally coined this term in 1710 in his book *Théodicée.* From the earliest of human writings, the sages have sought to bring clarity to the challenge of human anguish within the providence of God. In fact, this theme is at the core of several Biblical writings (e.g. Job and Habbakuk) as well as the works of Augustine of Hippo, Irenaeus, Origen and other early church leaders.[15]

If the God of love is completely good and incomparably powerful, why does suffering exist?

As an emergency services chaplain and as a pastor for over forty years, I have been given the privilege of serving and comforting people in some of their most dire situations. Whether sitting at the bedside of a precious saint under the care of hospice, helping after a school shooting, attending to responders in New York during 9/11, or counseling a troubled marriage, there is something very central

15 See Bibliography for helpful resources on theodicy.

to the pain and suffering of a broken world—I have been assured that God is present in our pain.[16]

At times there are no words to ease the hurt of another's loss as I sit alongside and weep with those who weep.[17] Piercing words like adultery, cancer, death, incest, rape, torture, terminal illness, suicide, terrorism or disaster depict horrors beyond human resolution and determination. And these are just some of the events in which God graciously intercedes and redeems within the pages of Scripture. The Lord reveals His compassion in the most appalling settings and consistently demonstrates that He will never leave us or forsake us. Even when our pain or anxieties become all-consuming, when the mind has a laser-lock on the fearful possibilities of what may lay ahead, He is present, peacefully leading us to His all-powerful perspective. Though not the author of our agony, God is near, reconciling our situations, no matter how cruel things may seem to be.

Scripture reveals that God has purpose in our brokenness.

Scripture reveals that God has purpose in our brokenness.[18] The Lord is able to bring clarity and perspective within our woes.[19] In eternity, God promises victory over temporal suffering.[20] We have assurance that Jesus Christ has personally experienced the depths of our pain.[21]

---

16 Hebrews 13:5.

17 Romans 12:15.

18 John 9:3.

19 2 Corinthians 1:1-8.

20 Romans 8:18.

21 Hebrews 2:9; Isaiah 53.

Sometimes our challenges are a result of spiritual attack, or the consequence of our own choices or actions.[22] Our traumatic experiences can lead to a transformed life, and at other times they can teach us major life lessons.[23] Throughout this book we will explore these various themes to discover that God, in all His goodness, has chosen the most glorious and gracious plan for His children. Considering the infinite possibilities and choices available to God in creating the world, He elected to display His glory and ultimate love through the cross of Jesus Christ. It is at the cross that all of God's majestic perfections are displayed in open triumph over death, pain, corruption and defiance. Jesus is both just and the Justifier within a slice of time in the midst of the expanse of eternity.[24] And it is there that God wants us to come by grace through faith to believe, to trust, and to be loved.

> "Come to Me, all you who labor and are heavy laden, and I will give you rest. Take My yoke upon you and learn from Me, for I am gentle and lowly in heart, and you will find rest for your souls. For my yoke is easy and My burden is light."[25]

In addition to focusing on a divine perspective in suffering, it is my goal to provide practical insights and experiences to help you grow in hope, help and healing. If you

22 Ephesians 6:10-20; Galatians 6:8; Deuteronomy 8:2.

23 cf. Genesis 50:20; Hebrews 12:11 ; James 1:2-4; Romans 5:1-5.

24 Romans 3:26.

25 Matthew 11:28-30 (NKJV).

are currently in a desperate time of pain or anguish and are gasping for relief, you will find here a foundation of solid action steps to guide you to transformation. Perhaps you are in a season where you are anxiously clinging to a thread of hope; or maybe at this moment you don't see any resolve at all. Know this, God is with you and He will use both divine and down-to-earth means to bring deliverance. And if at times you are overwhelmed and don't see any way out of your situation, be assured there is help on the way as you continue to read and receive the encouragements to come. Your feelings and thoughts, no matter how complex, are probably quite normal given what you are going through. No matter what situation you find yourself in at this moment, know for sure that *God is now here.* "For I know the thoughts that I think toward you, says the LORD, thoughts of peace and not of evil, to give you a future and a hope."[26]

Holding on Tight: Things to Consider

At the end of each chapter, practical encouragements and suggestions will be provided for your reflection and application in relation to the stresses that may come your way. In addition to the strengthening of one's faith, there are many down-to-earth practices that assist in helping with resistance, resiliency, and

26 Jeremiah 29:11 (NKJV). The context of this verse is when Jeremiah sent these words in a letter from Jerusalem to the remainder of the elders who were carried away captive to Babylon.

recovery when faced with life's challenges.[27] It is the Holy Spirit who comes alongside you in times of need to provide hope, healing, and comfort during hardship. In addition, He may lead you to consider adjustments in how you are choosing to live. It is in these applications that I trust that you will be strengthened in the depth of your soul as you lean into your difficulties and are gripped by God's grace and wisdom.

27 Following the tragedy of 9/11 an academic study was done to discover what helped people cope after this horrific crisis. Respondents affirmed that the three most important elements that assisted their distress were: (1) talking with others, (2) drawing upon their faith in God, and (3) connecting with their supportive groups (i.e. friends and family). Source: "A National Survey of Stress Reactions After the Sept. 11, 2001, Terrorist Attacks." *The New England Journal of Medicine, Vol. 345, No. 20. Nov. 2001.*

CHAPTER ONE

If the World Didn't Suck, We'd All Fall Off

There are life-defining moments that occasionally awaken us to the stark reality that life can seem to be quite unfair. Circumstances and people can at times appear so cruel, to the point of potentially shattering one's belief about providence and goodness. Yet it is within these very conditions that I have found some of the most fertile soil for meaning and transformation. I have always thought it odd that manure enables the earth to produce a bountiful crop. But it was a bumper sticker on the crinkled hind side of a car that led me to stumble further into a metaphor that challenged my perceptions of the order of universe—"If the world didn't suck, we'd all fall off."

Now at the outset I may have offended some of you by actually using the word "suck" in a book that connects with the complexities of God and human suffering—it is not a very dignified word. But then, from another point of view, gravity does have a downside. For those not offended by my slurping jargon, you may instead be gagging at my weak attempt at humor. Candidly, I realize that I will most likely offend more than a few as we engage together on a journey that will hopefully crush our pride and destroy the dainty etiquette of false platitudes of an explainable, finite God.

A number of years ago I spoke at a marriage enrichment dinner and was asked to have the couples participate in an interactive discussion. Within this assignment I wanted to encourage the couples to reflect upon their early courtship years. When counseling engaged couples just prior to their wedding ceremony, I often give the assignment of having them share from their hearts what they most love about each other and why they desire to spend the rest of their lives together. Tears often flow when these prenuptials are expressed to one another as couples have an opportunity to rehearse their covenantal love as a foundation for future bliss. In reflection of this exercise, I gave a similar opportunity at the marriage enrichment dinner for individuals to mutually share from their hearts a renewal of their remembrances and vows. Though many of the men were fidgety at first, romance eventually dominated the moment as smiles and embraces multiplied throughout the room.

In the most despairing situations, Jesus brings unique enlightenment that can profoundly transform our perspectives.

Months later to my surprise, I received the following letter from one of the wives who was in attendance that evening. It was a letter I immediately brought before the

Lord in deep intercession and prayer. It exemplified people's painful experiences that inevitably rocked me to my core.

> "You spoke at our married couples' dinner a couple of months ago. You had us tell each other what we loved best about our spouse. My husband, who has a challenge in sharing his feelings, found it difficult at the time to say much, but on the way home he told me that he was so proud of me. He shared that he never could have known what a wonderful mother and wife I would be and that he loved me. Who would have guessed that in just three short weeks after that night our 8½-month old baby was to die in a drowning accident? The most difficult part for me was my feelings of absolute failure as a mother. For 13 years mothering had been my identity because we have three other children. I really wanted to die. But God has most graciously picked me up and has truly given me His promised Comforter, and the words that came back to me were the ones I most needed to hear and they were from that night of the couples' dinner. The words from my husband, 'I never could have known what a wonderful mother and wife you would be.' I needed those words. They spoke truth when it was so easy to believe a lie."

This amazing mother discovered the foundation of strength and consolation that can only be described as divine, a rich, deep faith that goes beyond words. Hers is a testimony of God's pervasive hope that echoes with the Lord's presence and His tender touch of grace. It stuns me that in the most despairing situations, Jesus brings unique enlightenment that can profoundly transform our perspectives. His light shines most brightly when circumstances are the most dark. Within the wonder of God's mysterious comfort, this mom was enabled to gain perspective, and in time she became an instrument to come alongside others in their seasons of loss. Once again the promise of 2 Corinthians 1:4-5 is dramatically expressed, not as a mere precept, but as a living hope multiplied through one's shared experience. I find it interesting that when Paul wrote this epistle, the church of Corinth was facing challenges and disruptions that I am sure were agonizing for the apostle. In fact, in this specific letter, Paul repeats the word "comfort/encourage" in its noun and verb forms twenty-nine times. Our mutual support for one another within our distresses is like medicine to the soul.

I was visiting a pastor friend who lives in the Midwest a few years back and over lunch I posed the question to him, "What do you love most about the ministry?" To no surprise he responded that he loved the people. Then I followed with the inquiry, "What is the hardest part of the ministry?" Without skipping a beat my friend quipped, "The people!" I would imagine that the Apostle Paul would have smiled at this response given his personal, and sometimes painful, acknowledgments throughout his epistles.[28] People need people. Essential to our being created in the

28 See Romans 16:3-16; Philippians 4:1-3; 1 Timothy 1:18-20; 2 Timothy 4:9-15.

image of God is our requisite to be in community with one another. Within crisis intervention terms, we refer to this as S.O.S.—Significant Others' Support. It is often observed that *hurting people, hurt people.* But in a similar fashion it can be said that *healing people, are healed with people.* These important basics are reflected in the "one anothers" of Scripture: We are exhorted to love one another, serve one another, pray for one another, comfort one another, forgive one another, and encourage one another.[29] A Swedish proverb affirms, "Shared joy is double joy; shared sorrow is half sorrow." The bottom line in any agonizing experience is that we need God and we need each other, and this fundamental fact becomes the outworking of the two greatest commandments, to love God and love others.[30]

Loving and supportive relationships are essential to our well-being.

Loving and supportive relationships, then, are essential to our well-being. My birth name has a unique relevance to this testament. Growing up in Southern California with the name Mickey has its benefits due to the proximity of a certain world-famous amusement park. Wherever I am, I have the urge to proclaim that it's the happiest place on earth. What's more, when I am introduced to new families I find such delight in watching young children's perplexed stares as they gawk at my ears in confusion. The comedy of my life is sometimes bound up in my name. My birth name is actually Claude Michael Stonier. My father was also a Claude. My grandfather was actually Walter Schmiedeberg

29 See Appendix B.

30 Matthew 22:36-40.

from German roots, and with such a name he had a hard time finding a woman who would take on his surname. As a result, he legally changed his name to that of an acquaintance—Stonier (pronounced Stone-Yer or Stone-Yay if you prefer). I'm so very grateful to my grandfather as I could have been named Claude Schmiedeberg, and I would be forever single. My wife of over thirty-five years is Karen, and her name literally means "Pure One." What a pairing God did for us, as Claude finds its Latin origin rooted in "Lame One." When people tease me saying, "You're such a clod,"—yep, that's me. But my most cherished name is conferred upon me by my grandchildren, "Boppa." And "Boppa" of course comes from the root word for "have fun spoiling the living daylights out of your grandkids."

Boppa's significance came to its ultimate realization on a fateful evening when I was babysitting my oldest granddaughter, Kennedy. Following a day of Chucky Cheese, beach play, and ice cream, I helped carry out the sacred evening rituals of this five-year-old cherub: teeth brushing, climbing into pajamas, reading Bible stories, and saying a closing prayer for the night. As Kennedy was propped up with pillows in her princess bed, draped by a sheer pink-laced canopy, her Boppa knelt beside her bed with hands folded and eyes closed, praying a final prayer of blessing for her family. As I continued my prayers I heard a slight rustling, and then sensed movement as my granddaughter leaned into me. To my surprise, she was suddenly kissing my cheek, causing my heart to burst with love, and so I asked, "What are you doing, silly?" The response I received immediately changed my last Will and Testament as Kennedy hugged me tightly and exclaimed, "I just love you Boppa." Of course I hugged her in return, promising her all of my wealth while kissing her forehead. After tucking her in for the night I walked out of her room with my face aglow from the presence of pure love. I was only a few steps down the hall when the Lord spoke to me through this joyous moment as He whispered, "Do you understand what I long for in your relationship with Me? In the simplicity of a child, love me as *Abba*!"

It is because of this metaphor-turned-reality that we are His treasured family that God rescues us throughout human history from the guilt and shame of our wounds and failures. God calls us His children through faith in Jesus Christ. As adopted heirs to His throne of grace, the canopy through which all of our heart's challenges are defined becomes visible within this familial promise. In a world where evil forces are at play to destroy, discourage, and divide, it is through our struggles and disappointments that the voice of our Father prevails, silencing all accusations and condemnations as He longs for us to draw close to His heart and to know Him as *Abba,* our "gracious and loving Daddy." God breathes His affection upon His beloved, "Yes, I have loved you with an everlasting love; therefore with lovingkindness I have drawn you."[31] It is in this place of family intimacy that God's comforts illuminate His gracious acceptance and providential care. It is within this holy place of God's cherished presence that I hope to journey with you together through these pages.

31 Jeremiah 31:3 (NKJV).

Along with King David we can confidently call upon God's assurances, "Unless the Lord had been my help, my soul would soon have settled in silence. If I say, 'My foot slips,' Your mercy, O Lord, will hold me up. In the multitude of my anxieties within me, Your comforts delight my soul."[32]

I have encountered countless individuals who have struggled in their Biblical identity in Jesus Christ. People sometimes blur the true nature of God's love and grace through the lens of their earthly parental experiences, perhaps because of their parent's abandonment, neglect or abuse. Through difficult hardships, these individuals can be tempted to blame God or become hardened to their core as they wrongly ascribe to their heavenly Father the flaws of their earthly parents. It is my earnest desire to petition you to take the risk of faith and trust the God of the Scriptures, embracing the truth of our Father's Word over and above the very real emotions—but false assumptions—one may feel during the anguish of the moment. It is an appeal to believe in the *certainty* of God's love exceedingly beyond the *circumstances* of one's challenges.

Such was exemplified to me when my family received a Christmas card from a dear friend who is challenged with a second bout with cancer. Following the torturous rounds of chemotherapy treatments and a full mastectomy, her cancer went into remission for a couple of years. However, the cancer returned within other vital organs, starting a whole new regiment of difficult choices and struggles. At the end of the year, we received these words from this

32 Psalm 94:17-19 (NKJV).

amazing family that seemed most sacred, given their life situation:

> "Joy. God's provision. Gratitude. Fullness. These words define our 2014. Yes, it was peppered with words like metastatic breast cancer, tumors and surgery, but the good ALWAYS overpowers the bad. The light drowns out the dark. God lives, so we have hope. We had this hope before this cancer thing. We have this hope during it and will most definitely have hope after it! And this is nothing of us, but only because we have an unchanging God. Circumstances change, but He stays the same. Our prayer this Christmas and throughout your New Year is that you too taste and know this peace in the name of Jesus... in every day, in every situation. 'Lord, you establish peace for us; all that we have accomplished you have done for us' (Isaiah 26:12 NIV)."[33]

Sadly, people in extreme distress have a tendency to withdraw from community. When in a severe crisis, people at times seek to avoid additional pain by disconnecting from friends and family, thus isolating themselves from the potential help they need. Especially when dysfunctional relational dynamics are involved, there can be even more isolation and avoidance of social relations. In these seasons, individuals tend to resort to medicating their anxiety through substance abuse or destructive behaviors that

33 The Neese Family Christmas Card 2014.

further complicates their current challenge. If this describes your situation or someone you know, it is essential that this futile cycle is broken by actively reaching out to a counselor, pastor, or professional who can actively engage you with the needed support. If you need a referral, call a Bible-teaching church immediately. If adequate resources are not available through the initial contact, keep calling other local agencies until the appropriate help is offered. It may also be helpful to seek a referral through pastoral guidance or a church-going friend.

Most painful situations are choiceless.

As a young adolescent, I began my own journey of pain and despair watching the slow death of my mother as she battled breast and lung cancer. Her demise sent me reeling and riddled me with many doubts and questions about God's existence. After my mom's passing, it was my older sister—and best friend—who took on the primary role as my surrogate mom. However, three years after my mother's death my sister was killed in a car accident. The feelings of loneliness, anxiety, insecurity, and fear resurfaced and became my familiar companions. It was within this sudden family tragedy that I was faced with the two potential paths of *bitter* or *better*; *God is nowhere* or *God is now here.* Fortunately, within God's grace, I was led onto a course of faith wherein a deep compassion grew in my heart to be present for people in times of their duress.

Most painful situations are choiceless; we often have no part in the initiation of our crisis events. But, how we respond to our circumstances presents many options in the development of who we become as a consequence of our pain. As a result of my family losses, there was birthed within me a yearning to one day have a large family. In fact, it was this deep fatherly conviction that led me to pursue graduate studies in the field of marriage and family.

With this as a backdrop, it is no mystery that my love grew for my then-future-wife, Karen, as I observed her teaching the children in our church's family ministry. Once married, we anticipated a large family together, but eventually we received medical information that my wife might not be able to have children. In consultation with her doctor, Karen began a series of medications seeking to initiate ovulation. Eventually we got pregnant, but early on she was rushed into surgery with a tubal pregnancy—and her left fallopian tube was removed. With our pregnancy chances halved, Karen still managed to get pregnant three more times. Unfortunately, we had two miscarriages and another tubal pregnancy (that did not require surgery).

We couldn't help but identify with the plights of Sarah, Hannah, and Elizabeth in the Scriptures.[34] It was natural to question our circumstances; were we being punished for past sins? Why was God holding back His blessing? Our dreams and hopes for family were dissolving; the disappointment was inescapable. There were many tears and emotional flare-ups throughout our seasons of loss. Our physician even advised us that we would most likely not be able to have children, and that we should consider adoption.

During this season I was a youth and family pastor (which seemed somewhat of a paradox at the time), and

---

34 Genesis 16:1, 18:10-15;1 Samuel 1:1-18; Luke 1:5-25, 57-58.

within God's providence we were open to this new direction. To our surprise, Karen got pregnant again, and this time she went full-term with the birth of our daughter, Shiloh. Two years later, my wife gave birth to our twins, Michael and Julia (named after my sister). Two years after that we had our youngest daughter, Madalene (named after my mother). At this point, with four children under the age of five, I almost brought my wife back in to see her doctor to beg him to make her the way she was before. Psalm 127 teaches that "Children are a gift from God; they are His reward. Children born to a young man are like sharp arrows to defend him. Happy is the man who has his quiver full of them."[35] Our quiver was now quivering. Through the ups and twists and turns of life, we have grown in our appreciation of the foresight of God's grace, which is forever transforming us to hold fast to His very real presence and promises. We had grown to realize that our hope wasn't centered in *having* children, but rather in *being* His children in learning to know and love Him as our *Abba*. It is this perspective that consistently settles our hearts to know that God is good, even when circumstances are not.

As you continue to read, you will most likely fall into one of the following general categories: (1) You are facing very real life-changing and heart-wrenching situations, and are looking for hope and guidance; (2) You have been through tough situations and are looking for kinship, encouragement, and perhaps even broader philosophical

35 Psalm 127:3-5 (TLB)

and Scriptural mandates for the path you have already chosen; or (3) You are in a time of peaceful calm and are getting the sense that you need to either enjoy this present moment, or perhaps it's time to batten down the hatches as you sense God is preparing you for some unknown storms ahead. It is in life's uncertainties that I venture to invite you to gain perspective as you hold on tightly to the Lord, so you won't fall off of this outrageously thrilling, spinning globe.

Holding on Tight: Things to Consider

GROWING IN GRACE: When in the midst of a trial, we are invited in the Scriptures to direct our thoughts towards the Lord. Verses on which to meditate:

- "Finally, brethren, whatever things are true, whatever things are noble, whatever things are just, whatever things are pure, whatever things are lovely, whatever things are of good report, if there is any virtue and if there is anything praiseworthy – meditate on these things."[36]
- "You will keep him in perfect peace, whose mind is stayed on You, because he trusts in You. Trust in the LORD forever, for in YAH, the LORD, is everlasting strength."[37]

36 Philippians 4:8 (NKJV).

37 Isaiah 26:3-4 (NKJV).

- "If then you were raised with Christ, seek those things which are above, where Christ is, sitting at the right hand of God. Set your mind on things above, not on things on the earth. For you died, and your life is hidden with Christ in God."[38]

PRACTICAL CONSIDERATIONS: Sometimes when we are working through a tough situation there is benefit in getting outside input. This helps to give us an opportunity to look at our challenges through another point of view. Guidance for reappraisal or reinterpretation of our stressors can be helpful. Below are some suggested options:[39]

- Consider counseling.
- Reach out to people who care.
- Meet regularly with your mentor or life coach.
- Connect with your faith-support community.
- Gain new or different perspectives (sometimes called "cognitive reframing").
- Seek a trusted individual's guidance.
- Engage your social support network.
- Talk, talk, talk to an attentive listener.
- Give yourself permission to feel bad and share your feelings with others.

38 Colossians 3:1-3 (NKJV).

39 See the International Critical Incident Stress Management Foundation www.ICISF.org for additional recommendations and resources.

CHAPTER TWO

Behind the Veil

Life is often unfair. As a result, there is a danger in becoming polluted by self-centered bitterness. When faced with injustice, God's prescript is to keep our eyes fixed on Him. The mystery and beauty of the Old Testament narrative is alive with lessons and illustrations for personal instruction and reflection. In my years of ministry, I have found great benefit from the wisdom that is revealed behind the veil of Israel's temple worship. I invite you to take a journey in the shadows of the Old Testament high priests as they approached God within the sacred place of veneration and awe.

After years of intense training and preparation, it was with great anticipation that the new high priest would have the privilege of entering into the Holy of Holies to sprinkle the blood of the sacrifice on the mercy seat above the Ark of the Covenant. He knew well what to expect through the rigors of his diligent studies before entering into the temple of God. His predecessors and mentors had labored for years to make sure he was equipped to conduct every nuance of his duties. Within this cube-shaped room behind the veil he would see the golden floor and walls, the Ark of the Covenant, and the two cherubim of beaten gold facing the mercy seat. Testifying to a miraculous history, within the ark was contained the tablets of stone given to Moses, a jar of manna, and the rod of Aaron. Only once a year, on the Day of Atonement, one human being was allowed to humbly enter into the Most Holy Place. With great reverence and wonder the high priest would be privileged to venture into this sacred domain amidst a consecrated fragrance of incense that was reserved only for God. The entire experience would be a hallowed time of ministry wholly to the Lord. The human benefit—atonement for sin—would need to be repeated annually.[40]

On the high priest's head was a turban and a gold plate held by a blue cord that was engraved with the words "Holiness to the Lord." Upon the hem of his garment were golden bells that "will be heard when he goes into the holy place before the Lord and when he comes out, that he may not die."[41] The intricate particulars of both the attire and the ministry duties were laid out in minute detail that the priests "do not incur iniquity and die. It shall be a statute forever to him and his descendants after him."[42] The role

40 For a study of prominent Scriptures related to the Biblical ministry behind the veil, see: Exodus 26:33-36; 28:29-43; 29:13-22; 30:6, 20-37; 36:35; 37:1-29; 39:25; 40:1-38; Leviticus 16:2-6, 17-34; 24:3-9; Numbers 4:5;1 Kings 6:1-38; Mark 15:38; Hebrews 9:1-10.

41 Exodus 28:35 (NKJV).

42 Exodus 28:43 (NKJV).

of high priest afforded great honor and responsibility, and demanded much piety, but at the same time it came with great trepidation.

One can only imagine the restlessness of that fateful morning when the day dawned for the high priest to fulfill this venerable duty. He had been warned that sometimes people die behind the veil and others come out mute. Perhaps with a spirit overflowing with worship and gratitude, or maybe a mind gripped with anxiety and apprehension, he would press forward cautiously moving through the very thick blue, purple and scarlet veil hung from twenty cubits above by golden clasps. In reading the Scriptures, it is quite probable that his imagination would have previously danced with the expectation of visions of the glimmering gold and the grandeur of God's glorious presence. Very mindful that his heart needed to be aligned in prayer with pure motives and reverence toward such a majestic moment, a host of emotions and excitement would most likely surge like a flood through his entire being. With a wisp of grace, the curtain would close behind him, and now for the very first time he would peer into the place to which his whole life was committed. And what would his gaze behold? Would it be the brilliance of gold reflections splashing from wall to wall and upon the Ark of the Testimony and the mercy seat awaiting his atoning work? I submit that what his senses would drink in at that very instant would be a startling contrast to what his mind had envisioned.

With great respect, I suggest that the reality of this most holy environment was aged by centuries of dust, dried blood and soot-stained angelic hosts. It is likely that there were cobwebs and many spiders scurrying about within this secured chamber, startling this privileged intruder. It is feasible that his mind would have been confused as he got a whiff of stagnant, musty air and that his vision would present the Ark and mercy seat layered with cracked, dirty-brown, dried blood. There had been centuries of ceremonies where layers upon layers of atoning blood would have been splattered on the floor and altar. Since the decree was that only the high priest entered this domain once a year, it is very unlikely that a cleaning service ventured behind the veil to polish and clean this inner sanctum. While careful to maintain a sense of wonder, and guarding his heart from doubt or disrespect, the priest's spirit might gasp and whisper, "This is it? This is the Holy of Holies?" I can imagine his hand jerking up quickly to cover his mouth to refrain from further utterances of dismay, his emotions transitioning from fear and awe to a surge of reservation, and perhaps even skepticism. The mystery of this moment is shared by many, who tread down a path where expectations of beauty and wonder are displaced by the harsh realities of a broken world. Many God-honoring servants, with the most divine intentions, are faced with this same challenge when they are frustrated by the stains of human failures, injustices and deceits. This is the ministry behind the veil.

Many tread a path where expectations of beauty and wonder are displaced by the harsh realities of a broken world.

No less startling is the similar trek made by countless others who have ventured behind the veil of contemporary ministry, where their expected visions of the divine were replaced by the very real experiences of tainted, musty and fractured humanity. It is that first occurrence when an energetic new ministry volunteer or a staff member witnesses a leader's sinful motive or attitude that gives birth to a seed of misperception and eventual criticism. Or it is the newlywed that after months of anticipated joy for marital bliss is awakened to the reality of conflict, dissension, and strange noises and smells. For others it is the longed-for career advancement that erupts with increased stresses and diminished rewards. In my own years of family and ministry, I have witnessed vainglory, narcissism, nepotism, covetousness, abusive authority, prideful motives, and graceless expectations—and these are just the shadows that I see in my own sinister flesh. I have learned that these same character flaws, when shown by others, are a quick excuse for me to displace my critical judgment onto them. It is amazing when I turn my head to squint at the slivers in the eyes of these offenders, how people have to jump aside to avoid being smacked by the plank protruding from my own eye! Yet it is this daily walk behind the many veils of human disappointments that confronts us with our own frailty and our desperate need of grace.

I have learned in my walk with Jesus that there are two questions we should never ask…

I have learned in my walk with Jesus that there are two questions we should never ask—although they are two of the most common questions that seem to come like a drizzle upon our minds nearly every day. They are subtle questions, and yet they are the very thoughts and words that have pierced through so many hearts to give birth to resentment and pride. I find these questions to be like nettles in my brain, pricking my thoughts when the injustices of others intrude into my world. And it is when our souls are frustrated that these two questions seem to bleed upon those around us, potentially polluting an entire family or community. Even the greatest of saints were not immune to these tempting morsels of misguided utterances. It is the Apostle Peter who asked the first question, and it was Baruch, who penned Jeremiah's prophesies, who asked the second:

> "Peter, seeing him, said to Jesus, 'But Lord, what about this man?' Jesus said to him, 'If I will that he remain till I come, what is that to you? You follow Me.'"[43]

Speaking personally to Baruch in response to his self-interest, God warned:

> "And do you seek great things for yourself? Do not seek them; for behold, I will bring adversity on all flesh."[44]

Question 1

"What about him (or her or them)?" When we really stop and contemplate all that God has done to forgive us of

---

43 John 21:21-22 (NKJV).

44 Jeremiah 45:5 (NKJV). It is interesting to note that God was speaking to Baruch through Jeremiah, but Baruch was given the honor to write his own rebuke in the pages of Scripture.

our sins, it is stunning. We deserve eternal separation from our Holy God because of our rebellion against Him. And yet, God loved us so much He sent Jesus into the world to pay the debt for our sin. Although we are forgiven and in relationship with God, we still find in our hearts a menacing prompting of the flesh to judge and condemn others for their sins.

Jesus told an astute parable about the unforgiving servant. The servant was forgiven of millions of dollars but wouldn't forgive his debtors of just a few bucks.[45] Why is it that our sins look so much worse on others?

One evening after work, my wife and I went for a walk on the beach. These are always such special times as we get to catch up on things and share about our day's activities. On this particular occasion, I was bothered by a situation where there were a number of injustices and favoritisms made apparent. As I started to spew out my criticism, my wife quickly brought me back down off my high horse and said, "Honey, you follow Jesus." What was comical was that the very next morning, a pastor friend relayed to me that he and his wife had gone on a walk the night before where he was stewing over the very same thing I was (though he wasn't aware of my struggle). His wife in similar fashion cut him off in the middle of his tirade and simply told him to keep his eyes on Jesus. It is God's grace that these two saintly women didn't get pulled into the cesspool of their husbands' emerging bitterness, but instead they gently guided us back in line through Jesus'

45 Matthew 18:21-35.

tender words of correction, "You follow Me."[46] It is no secret that the husband often sees himself as the head of the house, but the wife is the neck, always turning the head back in the right direction.[47]

There are many times when life and ministry seem unfair, yet I'm often reminded of God's encouragement through the prophet Ezekiel where we learn that His ways are not unfair, but it is our ways that are unfair.[48] God's ways are so far above our ways, and His thoughts are far above our thoughts.[49] We are so limited in our perspectives in life's circumstances. In truth, only the omniscient and omnipresent God has all the facts.

In truth, only the omniscient and omnipresent God has all the facts.

Even King David realized that some of life's challenges were beyond his comprehension. When David penned Psalm 131, I can only imagine he also struggled with the injustices of life. I get the sense that David humbly learned that his perspective, even as king, was limited, and that he needed to entrust all judgments to the Lord:

> "LORD, my heart is not haughty, nor my eyes lofty. Neither do I concern myself with great matters, nor with things too profound for me. Surely I have calmed and quieted my soul, like a weaned

---

46 John 21:22 (NKJV).

47 I would imagine that it was the Apostle Peter's wife that helped him get on track as well. Peter's wife ministered by his side (1 Corinthians 9:5). Clement of Alexander reports that Peter's wife was martyred before him, and that the apostle encouraged her as she was led to her death. (Anti Nicene Father Clement ANF 2.541, c. 195) Perhaps it was her example that prepared the apostle for his eventual fulfillment of Jesus' prophetic words in John 21:18-19.

48 Ezekiel 18:25.

49 Isaiah 55:8-9.

child with his mother; like a weaned child is my soul within me."[50]

What peace we have when we come to the conclusion that there are some things that are perhaps too high for us, and we can commend these frustrations to the Lord. When you feel your heart surge to burst forth with the question, "what about…?," let the Holy Spirit quiet your soul as you trust Him to make things right—and then simply follow Jesus.

Question 2

From Baruch we learn the second question, "What about me?" In reality, this question is really the same question as the first, but asked from a subtle root of pride. It is not as overt in attacking others, but is instead the perverse poison of promoting oneself: "What about my needs?", "What's in it for me?", "Why didn't I get…?" In response to our query, God sighs, "Do you seek great things for yourself? Do not seek them."[51]

Though asked in a variety of ways, this folly comes down to the same self-centered core where sin is birthed. Even Satan's fall found its origin in the assertion, "I will!" "I will ascend into heaven, I will exalt my throne above the stars of God; I will also sit on the mount of the congregation on the farthest sides of the north; I will ascend above the heights of the clouds, I will be like the Most High."[52]

50 Psalm 131:1-2 (NKJV).

51 Jeremiah 45:5 (NKJV).

52 Isaiah 14:13-14 (NKJV).

Some call it egocentrism. Others call it narcissism. It is also labeled anthropocentrism (I want to impress you with all the big words I know). These are all variant terms describing the extremely destructive reality of pride. It is this very issue that corrupts a leader. It is this seemingly chronic trait that dissolves families. It is disguised and covered up by many other vices, but ultimately it is sin at its basic root.

But what is God's heart towards the darkness of people's hearts? Is He full of wrath and fury? Is He strategically waiting for a time to annihilate the filth of His creation? Consider God's perspective when He sees the wayward life:

> "I was crushed by their adulterous heart which has departed from Me, and by their eyes which play the harlot after their idols; they will loathe themselves for the evils which they committed in all their abominations. And they shall know that I am the LORD."[53]

It breaks God's heart that such a self-centered perspective leads people to self-loathing and separation from all the blessings that God had intended for them.[54]

These two questions easily surge to the forefront of our motives when we're befuddled with the troublesome circumstances that invade our lives. The temptation, so subtle and often unnoticed, is to blurt out: "What about him/her?", "What about me?" or "This is unfair!" When this dark, enticing cloud comes upon you, simply pray, "I will

53 Ezekiel 6:9-10 (NKJV).

54 Matthew 6:33.

follow Jesus!" Always LOOK UP as opposed to looking at others and yourself. When your eyes are on Him, your soul will be quieted and your heart will find a place of perfect peace:

> "You will keep him in perfect peace, whose mind is stayed on You, because he trusts in You. Trust in the LORD forever, for in YAH, the LORD, is everlasting strength."[55]

Have you ever noticed that sorrow, regret, and guilt are birthed from *looking back*, that worry and anxiety come from *looking ahead*, that doubt and despair result from *looking around at the circumstances*, but it is faith that *looks UP?* My wife once again turned my head (which she does quite often) to notice a friend's Facebook post that is quite relevant here, "Yesterday is a canceled check, tomorrow is a promissory note and today is cash in hand. Spend it wisely."[56] And may I pointedly notify you of the huge debit on your account to remind you that life is not about you, it is about Him.

My brother-in-law, Ken, enjoyed one of these "death-to-self moments" while heading home after work one afternoon. It was just a simple four-way stop that revved his emotions to full throttle. Driver's Education 101 teaches

---

55 Isaiah 26:3-4 (NKJV).

56 Art Rust, Jr. signed off his WABC (New York City) sports talk radio show with: "Yesterday is a canceled check. Tomorrow is just a promissory note. Today is the only time we have, so spend it wisely. Goodnight, Edna baby." (Rust's wife, Edna, died in 1986, after which he began this signoff.) "'Tomorrow' is a promissory note without a date" is cited in print by at least 1916, written by Henry Kaufman. A more complete version was printed in 1922: "Today is all you have. Tomorrow is a promissory note, and Yesterday is a canceled check. Act Today!" The author of the full phrase is unknown, but it's been credited to George Bernard Shaw, Hubert Tinley and Kay Lyons.

us that when two cars pull up to an intersection at the same time, the driver on the right has the right of way. However, in this instance it wasn't even close as the trespasser on the left totally ignored the stop sign and just rolled forward out of turn and abruptly navigated left onto Ken's road. Of course, my godly brother-in-law quickly forgave and fell in line behind this obviously errant driver. But this momentary peace was eventually supplanted by a growing frustration when the man in front of him drove at a pace far below the speed limit. Now, any rational observer knows that the laws of equity dictate that if a person breaks the Law of Stop, they are obligated to break the Law of Speed. Naturally, Ken followed his impulse to try to pass this roadblocker.

Though initially he was hindered during his passing attempts, eventually Ken "The Flash" made a quick move and passed his nemesis. Taking advantage of the moment, he had the opportunity to actually look into the eyes of his foe while smiling and pointing his index finger with a scolding gesture (yes, just the index finger). This little jab became the spark that ignited an ensuing road rage escapade, complete with fast and furious bumper-to-bumper accelerations throughout the community. Ken realized that this was getting out of control and that he was nearing his destination. With emotions subsiding, he mentally surveyed his options and decided to take the humble direct approach. Inadvisably, he pulled up to his home, exited his car, and stood in his driveway awaiting his rival. As expected, a red-faced adversary leapt from his vehicle with his chest inflated and fists clenched. Taking initiative, Ken quickly waived his arms, calling for a truce as he exclaimed, "Hey man, I'm so sorry for upsetting you. I shouldn't have done that. You see, I'm a Christian and I want to apologize." Upon hearing this declaration, the man immediately dropped his head, shrugged his shoulders and sighed, "I'm a Christian, too." The two humiliated new acquaintances quickly shook hands and exchanged further apologies that concluded with an invite from my brother-in-law to share a snack inside together.

Being right can actually lead one to being *dead right.*

Throughout this incident, Ken honestly felt that he was in the right and that justice demanded vindication. But being right can actually lead one to being *dead right*. Why is it that we are voracious for entitlement when we feel justified, but we are so blind to *our* failures and *our* need for grace? How are we to navigate through the injustices that are thrown upon us with the expectation that we should be quick to forgive? Truly our *uplook* determines our *outlook*—but oftentimes the pain of being sharply poked makes us want to close our eyes altogether.

"Forgive and forget," we've been told; however, I have come to realize that forgetfulness only comes with brain trauma or growing old. Forgiving is the important part of that phrase, thank God—we may never forget the hurts that others may have inflicted upon us, but God faithfully empowers His children to experience the healing power of forgiveness.

Unforgiveness is a cancer of the soul that slowly spreads like a plague, damaging one's physical health, emotions, social relationships, and spiritual vitality. Many are completely unaware that the many maladies of life they are experiencing are entirely rooted in unforgiveness. The fruit of this condition will give birth to constant anxiety, insecurity, fear, anger, or nagging doubt. If you sense a tinge of conviction in your heart, it is crucial that you take immediate action to connect with a respected individual who will talk candidly and speak truth into your life without holding back. Pause right now and pray this prayer:

> "Lord, reveal to me my lack of forgiveness and the sources of my pain. In Jesus' name I ask for Your authority of love and mercy to cleanse my heart and mind from bitterness and resentment. Restore to me the joy of Your Holy Spirit, and lead me into an accountability relationship where my true identity in Jesus Christ is affirmed. Forgive me now for clinging to my hurt rather than receiving to Your healing grace. In Jesus' name, I am now free to walk in Your forgiveness. Amen!"

A follow up to your prayer may be getting counsel and affirmation in relation to your actions of forgiveness. There is great freedom in sharing with others about your release from bitterness. Forgiveness may seem impossible, but it is essential to know that when we don't have the power or ability to actively pursue forgiveness, we can give this burden to God Who enables us to experience Jesus' forgiveness through the work of the cross. When we are faithless, God is faithful to meet us in our areas of weakness to transform our hearts into His heart for those He was crucified for. "Father, forgive them, for they know not what they do."[57]

A beautiful resolve to this dilemma is found in the footsteps of Jesus. I ask you once again to venture past the veil and to allow God to put your ego on the altar of His grace as you engage actively in the Lord's healing. It is there that you will hurt badly and yet love deeply. It is there that the two self-asserting questions that spring from personal injustice or indignation will dissolve within the ultimate question, "What about Jesus?"

Holding on Tight: Things to Consider

GROWING IN GRACE: God's grace is at the foundation of all of our spiritual disciplines. It is within grace that the means of faith and Biblical practices are empowered by God to transform the heart. Take time this week to ponder these rich encouragements from Scripture:

> "And God is able to make all grace abound toward you, that you, always having all sufficiency in all things, may have an abundance for every good work."[58]

> "For it is by grace you have been saved, through faith–and this is not from yourselves, it is the gift of

57 Luke 23:34 (ESV).

58 2 Corinthians 9:8 (NKJV).

God–not by works, so that no one can boast. For we are God's handiwork, created in Christ Jesus to do good works, which God prepared in advance for us to do."[59]

"Therefore, since we are receiving a kingdom which cannot be shaken, let us have grace, by which we may serve God acceptably with reverence and godly fear."[60]

"Each of you should use whatever gift you have received to serve others, as faithful stewards of God's grace in its various forms."[61]

"You therefore, beloved, knowing this beforehand, take care that you are not carried away with the error of lawless people and lose your own stability. But grow in the grace and knowledge of our Lord and Savior Jesus Christ. To Him be the glory both now and to the day of eternity. Amen."[62]

PRACTICAL CONSIDERATIONS: People that bounce back more quickly after a difficult challenge have a number of common factors that assist their coping. Below is a list of strengths that are shared among people that tend to be more resilient in their trauma recovery. They:

---

59 Ephesians 2:8-10 (NIV).

60 Hebrews 12:28 (NKJV).

61 1 Peter 4:10 (NIV).

62 2 Peter 3:17-18 (ESV).

- Are generally in good wellbeing and health in terms of their physiological, psychological, sociological, emotional and spiritual priorities.
- Tend to be effective problem solvers in how they understand their challenges, explore options and solutions, and identify a follow-through plan.
- Are mature and responsible in actively developing positive lifestyle choices.
- Maintain a healthy sense of humor.
- Have a strong social support network.
- Have a clear sense of meaning and purpose for their life.
- Develop an ongoing growth plan in their faith perspectives.
- Actively display a concern for others through their engagement in service projects.
- Nurture ongoing positive interpersonal skills.
- Tend to have a personal competence in their learning and adapting to change.
- Have a high reliance on God and a sense of self-worth.
- Have the ability to refocus after a challenge and move forward with proper adjustments.
- Maintain healthy boundaries over their priorities and essential relationships.
- Take responsibility for their recovery and avoid the "victim" mentality–this is sometimes enhanced through counseling.
- Are able to integrate the trauma into their current life story without excessive emotional discomfort or collapse.

CHAPTER THREE

Warning Signs

God gives us warning signs. When we are living outside of the bounds of His precepts, we begin to reap the fruit and consequences of our choices. It is wise to take heed of these warning signs and surrender to the example of Jesus Christ. As a police and fire department chaplain, I frequently participate in ride-alongs where I support the emergency responders and community members in times of crisis. Many of the 911 calls tend to be medical aid responses. Of distinction was one early Saturday morning call from a resident in Southeast San Diego, where a man in his late forties was experiencing chest pains.

When the crew entered the small duplex, one could discern that there must have been a wild party the previous night by the remnant of bottles and the disarray of the house. The initial scene was startling to me as I took in the surroundings, only to see a half-naked overweight gentleman puffing on a cigarette, complaining of a possible heart attack. The paramedic was quick to take charge of the situation as he attached monitors and initiated a series of questions:

"On a scale of one to ten, with ten being intensely severe, what level of pain are you feeling?" probed the medic.

The man responded, "It's like an eight. I feel like a car is on my chest."

The ensuing questions came rapid fire, "Are you taking any medication?"

"Yes, for angina pectoris," came the response. (Angina pectoris is a chest discomfort due to poor blood flow through the blood vessels in the heart.)

"When did you last take your prescription?"

The man confessed that his prescription had run out and that he hadn't gotten around to having it refilled.

"Does your family have a history of heart disease?" asked the medic.

"Yes, my dad died of a heart attack when he was forty-eight."

"How old are you?" was the obvious next question.

By this time, I was not surprised to hear his reply, "I'm forty-nine."

"Are you on a diet and exercise plan?"

With head hanging down he responded, "Uh, no, I'm not good with that stuff."

The paramedic then observed, "Looks like you had a celebration last night—are you a heavy drinker?"

"Not really, just sort of a party guy," came his reply.

As I was listening to this exchange, I couldn't help thinking that if there was a checklist of how to die before your fiftieth birthday, this guy had successfully checked off every item on the list.

Things reached a climax when the crew put the man on a gurney to transport him to the hospital. At that moment panic set in and the patient grabbed hold of the paramedic's shirt, and with eyes as big as saucers exclaimed, "Don't let me die!" Though I was quietly praying for this individual, I found it so odd that someone could live completely contrary to life's wisdom, and then beg for a different outcome from his chosen course. This incident has lingered with me for years, as I am often a witness to the regrets of many people who have ignored the prudence of God in the pursuit of their own frivolity. I have discovered that people routinely ignore the warning signs that are God's gracious admonitions.

I am often a witness to the regrets of many people who have ignored the prudence of God in the pursuit of their own frivolity.

We are instructed in Paul's encouragement to the Galatians that the fruit of the Spirit is "Love, joy, peace, forbearance, kindness, goodness, faithfulness, gentleness and self-control."[63] In harmony with Paul, the Apostle James wrote, "But the wisdom that comes from heaven is first of all pure; then peace-loving, considerate, submissive, full of mercy and good fruit, impartial and sincere."[64]

63 Galatians 5:22-23 (NIV).

64 James 3:17 (NIV).

The principle of sowing and reaping is a fact of life. When you live within the realm of God's grace, you will find harmony within His will that bears the fruit of His spiritual bounty of love, joy, peace and kindness. When you sow to your arrogance and carnality, you will instead reap a harvest of frustration and ruin. The virtues of the Spirit provide a very clear gauge by which we can monitor our transformative growth. I have found that when the warning signs of anger, cynicism, selfish ambition, contention, envy and pride leak out of my life, I have begun to follow a course toward my own demise.

The fruit of the Spirit should always be the monitor by which we diagnose the state of our heart.

Even the good pursuits within a busy life will yield a crop of polluted attitudes, behaviors, words, and motives if they are unbalanced by the refinement of abiding in Christ's presence. Have you ever noticed that exhaustion is not listed as one of the fruits of the Spirit? Don't get me wrong, I am not advocating slothfulness in our pursuits, or challenging the "hard-work" ethic. However, when your interactions become harsh, abrupt, or even cruel, no matter how good your intentions might be, these are warning signs that your heart is murmuring with carnality. The fruit of the Spirit should always be the monitor by which we diagnose the state of our heart. The essential question will forever be, "Does it look and sound like Jesus?"

As in the case of our ride-along patient, people frequently justify their defiance of what's best for them, dismissing the warning signs through a series of rational defenses. Our subtle—yet quite deadly—self-protective delusions will corrupt the heart to reason away our misguided assumptions. Six of these devices are:

Denial – *"I don't have a problem."*
Justification – *"I am in the right."*
Blame – *"It's their fault."*
Rationalization – *"I can't help it."*
Projection – *"Everyone's doing it."*
Indifference – *"I can't do anything about it."*

Though painful, you will find it wonderfully healing to experience the Christ-like sacrifice of confronting injustices or mistakes openly and humbly, without any move towards deflection.

At the foundation of this discussion is Peter's reassurance to God's beloved church during an era of horrendous persecution under Cesar Nero.

> "Beloved, I beg you as sojourners and pilgrims, abstain from fleshly lusts which war against the soul, having your conduct honorable among the Gentiles, that when they speak against you as evildoers, they may, by your good works which they observe, glorify God in the day of visitation.
>
> Therefore submit yourselves to every ordinance of man for the Lord's sake, whether to the king as supreme, or to governors, as to those who are sent by him for the punishment of evildoers and for the praise of those who do good. For this is the will of

> God, that by doing good you may put to silence the ignorance of foolish men—as free, yet not using liberty as a cloak for vice, but as bondservants of God. Honor all people. Love the brotherhood. Fear God. Honor the king.
>
> Servants, be submissive to your masters with all fear, not only to the good and gentle, but also to the harsh. For this is commendable, if because of conscience toward God one endures grief, suffering wrongfully. For what credit is it if, when you are beaten for your faults, you take it patiently? But when you do good and suffer, if you take it patiently, this is commendable before God. For to this you were called, because Christ also suffered for us, leaving us an example, that you should follow His steps: 'Who committed no sin, nor was deceit found in His mouth'; who, when He was reviled, did not revile in return; when He suffered, He did not threaten, but committed Himself to Him who judges righteously; who Himself bore our sins in His own body on the tree, that we, having died to sins, might live for righteousness—by whose stripes you were healed."[65]

These verses dramatically assist the Christ-follower in navigating through the imbalances in life. As noted previously, there are many circumstances that just aren't fair. I have found these precepts from the Apostle Peter to be

65 1 Peter 2:11-24 (NKJV).

essential to my own growth in the joys of life, liberty and the pursuit of Jesus. When I find myself challenged by my injured feelings or situations I don't find just, I cling to these verses as encouragements for my empathy. And of course if anything is truly unfair, it is that God sent His only Son, Jesus Christ, to die for us while we were yet sinners. Grace is unfair, and I'm so thankful that God wasn't fair in dealing with my sin.

Grace is unfair, and I'm so thankful that God wasn't fair in dealing with my sin.

Here's the deal: throughout our lives, we run into countless situations where people and situations upset us. We will experience actions and words that are done and said that are just flat-out hurtful. Our natural tendency is to defend ourselves, and at the expense of others, to put people in their proper place. Many find themselves living in a daily battle, fighting for their rights to maintain the uprightness of their situation and their pursuit of personal happiness.

This especially happens in marriage. Research shows that couples tend to relate to one another on a basis of fairness, otherwise known as Social-Equity Theory. Though not always intentional, people will treat others as they have been treated. It is the sense that if you are nice to me, then I'll be nice to you. If you are harsh or cruel, then I don't have to be kind either. In a naturalistic sense, people tend to relate to one another on a contractual basis. If you hold up your end of the bargain, then I'll hold up my end. A contract upholds justice, but we must all be grateful that God dealt with us according to His covenant, which testifies of grace. Justice is getting what you deserve. Mercy is not getting what you deserve. Grace is getting the blessings of what we don't deserve.

Sociological studies show that people tend to greatly overestimate the benefits they bestow upon others, and underestimate the harm they do to others. In addition, we also tend to intensify our experience of the pain inflicted upon us by others. These tendencies provide evidence of our fallen human nature, where apart from Christ, we focus our perception from the viewpoint of the self. People generally have a self-centered orientation to the world around them.

Apart from Christ, I tend to evaluate situations on the basis of how they affect ME.

Apart from Christ, I tend to evaluate situations on the basis of how they affect ME. If there is a conflict, I am compelled to protect ME by projecting that YOU are the problem. I may even acknowledge that I have a part in this conflict, but it is really YOU that is at fault. This is nothing new, of course; it all started in the Garden of Eden in Genesis 3. God speaks to the man, who blames the woman, who blames the serpent. Thousands of years later, James points out the same trouble: "Where do wars and fights come from among you? Do they not come from your desires for pleasure that war in your members? You lust and do not have. You murder and covet and cannot obtain. You fight and war. Yet you do not have because you do not ask."[66]

A few years ago at a young adult Bible study at our house I asked the ladies to describe the perfect man. The

66 James 4:1-2 (NKJV).

list grew quickly to picture a man who would be humble, Godly, gracious, attentive, sacrificial, attentive, kind, joyful and loving. Then I asked the girls whom they had just described. And of course they were depicting Jesus Christ. It is not hard to figure out that when you are moving in the direction of the qualities of Jesus you are moving in the direction of what produces the authentic life. What takes us away from that target also takes us in a direction that keeps us from experiencing the fruit of His life. The more you are focused on being centered on Jesus Christ, the more dynamic you will experience the ultimate purpose of being. To have a Christocentric life is the authentic perspective in which a person should live.[67] All things are compared to Him and not to ME.

When you want to build a structure or a wall, you need to make sure the cornerstone is accurately placed. Everything else will be arranged and positioned from that first stone, so it is vital that it is in its proper place. It is no wonder that Jesus is declared to be our primary cornerstone from which all else derives its meaning and significance:

> "Now, therefore, you are no longer strangers and foreigners, but fellow citizens with the saints and members of the household of God, having been built on the foundation of the apostles and prophets, Jesus Christ Himself being the chief cornerstone, in whom the whole building, being fitted together, grows into a holy temple in the Lord, in

67 "Christocentric" is a theological term within Christianity that esteems Jesus Christ as central to a person's life and worldview.

whom you also are being built together for a dwelling place of God in the Spirit."[68]

You will find 1 Peter 2 to be a very helpful guide for you to get ME out of the center of your perspectives. To walk in Jesus' steps and to do what Jesus would do, at its very core, is to give up your *rights* and to let God be *right*. Our outlook should be that no matter how unfair things may seem, we must commit and entrust ourselves "to Him who judges righteously."[69] In other words, we should live within the contentment of knowing that we serve an audience of One. We should thrive with the viewpoint that God sees all, and that what matters is that we live in the mindset that God will work all things according to His perfect will and plan. We can let go of the controls and experience our surrender to His good will and pleasure.

It is an enigma that our times of brokenness can be so peaceful within His fullness.

In addition, take notice that in 1 Peter 3:1,7 the key word "likewise" connects how we relate to one another in marriage. "Likewise" finds its direct context back in 1 Peter 2:23 where couples are challenged to commit themselves "to Him who judges righteously." If you pray about making this perspective the core of all that you do in relation to others, you will be growing in Christlikeness in ways that take you to the very cornerstone of your faith. If you live by this precept, you will find that your life aligns in

68 Ephesians 2:19-22 (NKJV).

69 1 Peter 2:23 (NKJV).

Jesus Christ with just about everything else. However, you will also discover that this can be one of the most difficult places to consistently abide.

Life happens all around us, and even in—especially in—the good times, we might be tempted to take our eyes off Jesus and be drawn back to ME. In the midst of our traumatic experiences, our troubles may cause worry, doubt, or self-pity. And yet, even in our darkest place, looking to Christ will refocus our attention on His justice, promises, and grace, realigning us to our cornerstone once again. It is an enigma that our times of brokenness can be so peaceful within His fullness.

Once again, we are invited to come die with Jesus, that we might be resurrected to live in Jesus. As the Apostle Paul affirms, "I have been crucified with Christ; it is no longer I who live, but Christ lives in me; and the life which I now live in the flesh I live by faith in the Son of God, who loved me and gave Himself for me."[70] I have found that when I feel the pains of injustice it is because I am not dead yet, since dead things don't get hurt. Oh what a mysterious joy it is when we are on our daily ride-along with Jesus. Assuredly, He must increase and we must decrease.[71]

Holding on Tight: Things to Consider

GROWING IN GRACE: In a hectic and busy world it is easy to miss some of the warning signs that God sends our way. The

70 Galatians 2:20 (NKJV).

71 John 3:30 (NKJV).

Scriptures give frequent instructions to God's people to slow down, rest, wait, and to be still. It is within the times of quiet that God often speaks through His still, small voice to awaken our hearts to potential pitfalls. Take fifteen minutes today to meditate upon the rich wisdom God gives you in the following verses:

- "He gives power to the faint, and to him who has no might he increases strength. Even youths shall faint and be weary, and young men shall fall exhausted; but they who wait for the LORD shall renew their strength; they shall mount up with wings like eagles; they shall run and not be weary; they shall walk and not faint."[72]
- "Commit your way to the LORD; trust in Him and He will do this: He will make your righteous reward shine like the dawn, your vindication like the noonday sun. Be still before the LORD and wait patiently for Him; do not fret."[73]
- "He says, 'Be still, and know that I am God; I will be exalted among the nations, I will be exalted in the earth.' The LORD Almighty is with us; the God of Jacob is our fortress."[74]
- "Come to Me, all you who labor and are heavy laden, and I will give you rest. Take My yoke upon you and learn from Me, for I am gentle and lowly in heart, and you will find rest for your souls."[75]

---

72 Isaiah 40:29-31 (ESV).

73 Psalm 37:5-7 (NIV).

74 Psalm 46:10-11 (NIV).

75 Matthew11:28-30 (NKJV)

PRACTICAL CONSIDERATIONS: Maybe you find yourself currently in a season of extreme pressure and anxiety. You feel like you are about to explode, that certain situations are sounding a load alarm of injustice. Or perhaps you are in a time where life is just basically crazy, or maybe you have experienced a terrible loss that overwhelms you. It is in these periods that sometimes the best thing to do is...nothing. Under the tyranny of the urgent, it is easy to make the error of contributing to your heavy load by not slowing down.[76] It is helpful to intentionally embrace leisure as you reduce the input of what tends to increase your stress arousal. Perhaps some of these suggestions might prove helpful to you:

- Take extra time for personal privacy to engage your devotional life.
- Consider setting time aside this week to enjoy some of your favorite spiritual disciplines (e.g. fasting, prayer, solitude, worship, simplicity, Bible meditation, study, memorization of Scripture, silence, frugality, and/or confession).
- Say "no" to additional requests that are coming your way that may unnecessarily add to your load.
- Monitor your days off; make sure you are taking them.
- Plan on taking some extended time off or vacation.
- Return to your normal schedule and routines where possible if things have gotten chaotic.
- Take a well-deserved nap.

76 A suggested encouragement is to read the brief booklet: Hummel, Charles. (1967) *Tyranny of the Urgent*. Intervarsity Press. Downers Grove, IL.

- Protect your sleep needs and make sure you are not diminishing your normal sleep hours as you seek to maintain regularity of rest.
- If experiencing reoccurring thoughts, dreams or flashbacks, these are normal in a crisis. They will generally decrease over time and become less painful.
- Give yourself grace.
- Don't label yourself as "weak" or "crazy" when you experience stress symptoms. You are responding normally and are having normal reactions to an abnormal challenge.
- Consider having a massage, sauna or soaking in a warm bath or Jacuzzi.
- Invest time in reading, hobbies, crafts, cooking or other enjoyable activities.
- Play with a family pet.
- Avoid overindulging with alcohol and stimulants trying to numb the pain.
- Drink plenty of water, as hydration is important.
- Be cautious on over-medicating with prescription drugs.
- Strengthen relationships and faith commitments.
- Listen to music that relaxes and refreshes you.

CHAPTER FOUR

The Azimuth Check

Little compromises have long-lasting, devastating results. Being *close* to the truth is not close enough. History is full of examples of secret indiscretions that have led to major tragedies. Recalibrating our course, even in seemingly insignificant circumstances of life, can lead to great benefit.

My family heritage goes back a few generations living in Southern California, and as such, we have always had an affinity for beach communities and ocean sports. When I was a child my dad told us that when he retired he wanted to move onto a sailboat. My mom was always up for the next fun challenge and she encouraged my dad to go for it. Her reasoning was that you shouldn't wait until you are old to do what you always wanted to do. So my parents sold our home in Hermosa Beach and moved our family onto the *Maramel*, a forty-five foot staysail schooner built in 1937. My memories from those early years are balanced between sailing adventures, Channel Island voyages, and throwing up a lot. It seems like the joys of life are always measured with a little hardship, especially for kids who frequently get seasick.

Each year we would enter the *Maramel* in the Newport-to-Ensenada Yacht Race. This annual 125-nautical-mile international competition is billed as the largest yacht race in the world. As a pre-adolescent I served as a deckhand (which meant I tried to stay out of everyone's way). We never won any awards, but it was always a thrill to take our home on an overnight cruise amidst thousands of other sailing vessels.

At the conclusion of one of these spring maritime exploits I learned one of life's vital lessons. At dawn when we should have been nearing our Ensenada destination, I was up early on the deck enjoying the morning sunrise. As I gazed east, I noticed off in the distance a mountain range I remembered as being just south of Ensenada. From my primitive analysis, I believed that we were swiftly sailing past the finish line and therefore I quickly brought my observation to my dad. His response was that I must have been mistaken but that he would use the sextant (our 1960's version of GPS) to double-check our location. To my father's surprise, indeed we were about six miles off course. When he recharted our original path my dad found out that our navigator had initiated us on a trek that was a couple of degrees off. One might think that one or two degrees off the mark doesn't matter that much; however, when you travel about 140 miles on a slightly altered angle, you will find yourself a considerable distance from where you wish to be.

The military has a helpful process in navigating missions that is termed the "azimuth check." An azimuth check is literally the discipline of realigning your coordinates at various points along your path to make sure you end up at your expected destination. I have found this concept to be very beneficial in traversing through life's sudden storms and abrupt challenges. It is during these seasons of life that we are given the opportunity to pause, reflect, and perhaps reset our course to make sure we don't drift from God's ultimate purposes. Whether it is attending a funeral service, struggling through a marital crisis, experiencing the birth of a first child, or even purchasing a new home, the highs and lows of our life's progress provide occasional azimuth checks to reevaluate our essential purpose. It is the upside of down and the downside of up that provide us the opportunity for a pause. In a sense, these reflective moments can be referred to as our eternal GPS—God's Positioning System.

One of these seasons came to King David in the aftermath of his many years of exile and warfare. "It happened in the spring of the year, at the time when kings go out to battle, that David sent Joab and his servants with him… But David remained at Jerusalem. Then it happened one evening that David arose from his bed and walked on the roof of the king's house."[77] Though we don't have the specific details of David's mindset, one can assume that after

77 2 Samuel 11:1-2 (NKJV).

all the years of war, loss of loved ones, injustices, and continual attacks, David had seemingly "hit the wall." Without trying to over-diagnose his behavior, David appeared to be struggling through a period of burnout. He was shirking his responsibilities as king to lead and to protect his people, he was not sleeping well, and his heart was most likely troubled.

In stress management we refer to these signs as the "D's" of burnout: depression, detachment, distancing, demoralization, depersonalization, defeatism and deadness. David had witnessed the death of tens of thousands of human beings. He had lived nearly a decade on the run. And upon coming into his kingdom after the death of his best friend, his peaceful overtures to the king of Ammon had been met with humiliation.[78]

I venture to say that David's plight was not an overnight moral collapse.

So there we find David alone on his rooftop, and eventually he gazed upon a beautiful woman as she bathed. Instead of turning away, David displaced his integrity and gave place to his lust. He inquired about the woman's identity and learned that she was Bathsheba, the wife of Uriah, one of his mighty warriors. Elsewhere, we discern that Bathsheba was also possibly the granddaughter of one of his advisors and close friends.[79] "Then David sent messengers and took her; and she came to him and he lay with

78 2 Samuel 10.

79 Bathsheba was the daughter of Eliam. In 2 Samuel 23:34 we learn that Eliam was the son of Ahithophel. This familial connection perhaps explains why Ahithophel took his life through suicide (2 Samuel 17) when Absalom rejected his counsel, knowing that once again David would succeed when Ahithophel wanted him dead.

her."[80] This act of adultery was followed by the intentional murder of Bathsheba's husband, David's loyal friend. How did a man after God's heart, the sweet psalmist of Israel, get so far off course?

I venture to say that David's plight was not an overnight moral collapse. Rather, I would suggest that there was an altered course, a few minor compromises during a season of duress that lead him on a path of complete compromise. It was David's sinkhole syndrome.[81] A sinkhole is often the result of a trivial leak in a pipe below the surface of the pavement. However, over time, that outflow slowly pulls away dirt, gravel, stones, and eventually boulders, to create a cavern just beneath the street above. Finally, and often unexpectedly, the weight of the life above violently collapses upon the void below, which simply began as an insignificant trickle. It's not hard to conclude that over a period of time, David had slowly drifted from his foundation of integrity and honor that had guided him through his many years of hardship. This course eventually led to a trail of great family suffering and anguish of heart.

In working alongside firefighters, I have observed that they tend to be very protective of their children's safety. When emergency responders' eight-year-olds are allowed to ride their bikes in the cul-de-sac, they are strapped down with kneepads, elbow pads, and a sturdy helmet. Their kids often complain about having to put on these layers of

---

80 2 Samuel 11:4 (NKJV).

81 For a classic resource on this concept, see *Ordering Your Private World* by Gordon MacDonald. Thomas Nelson, Inc., 1984.

protective gear since they are just riding in the immediate neighborhood. Why such an extreme insistence on safety? As you can imagine, it is because the firefighters have been to too many incidents where a child is laying on the street unconscious because he fell off his bike and wasn't wearing a helmet. A surge of frustration boils up within the hearts of medics as these extreme injuries could have been averted if the parents had taken more precautions.

In a similar fashion, as a pastor for many years, I have witnessed the senseless harm and devastation that happens in people's lives when they accept minor compromises that are excused as being only a couple degrees away from where they know they should be. After all, people assume, at least they are not as far off course as other people they know. But given time: that six-pack becomes a series of glasses topped off with harder liquor; that minor glance here and there results in extended times on a computer or smart phone visiting pornography sites; that bout of anger goes unchecked and eventually grows into rage and domestic violence. At times these compromises are attempts to simply drown one's pain through self-indulgent behaviors, or to vent the pent-up frustrations of deep wounds. These capitulations begin as supposedly insignificant trickles, but eventually they collapse families or crush one's future integrity. Such was the story of King David. But fortunately, his testimony didn't end without a friend's confrontation.

Socrates is reputed to have said, "The unexamined life is not worth living." It is true that the virtues of one's character are often strengthened through times of contemplation and personal examination. This discipline of personal reflection in God's presence has the potential to bring deep-seated depravity to the surface. The Scriptures provide a plethora of examples of individuals who did not finish well because of subtle compromises. Paul warned, "Now these things became our examples, to the intent that we should not lust after evil things as they also lusted… Now all these things happened to them as examples, and they were written for our admonition, upon whom the ends of the ages have come. Therefore let him who thinks he stands take heed lest he fall."[82] The philosopher, Santayana, perceived, "He who does not remember the past is condemned to repeat it." And the well-known definition of insanity is doing the same things over and over while expecting different results.[83] The appeal of wisdom is to be attentive to the warnings of the failed lives from the past and to heed the voices of friends and family who seek to confront us of the potential peril in the present. Such was the blessing that painfully came to David that awakened him from his delusion—from living a lie.

> The fall into moral ruin of many great leaders often occurs following closely behind some of their greatest successes.

Driven by God's grace, Nathan the prophet was given the monumental and somber task of confronting David's entitlement and concealed sin. Not too many years earlier, Nathan delivered God's Messianic prophecy to the king,

82 1 Corinthians 10:6, 11-12 (NKJV).

83 A concept attributed to Albert Einstein as quoted *The New Yorker* (1925).

that through David's lineage the eternal kingdom would be established.[84] Upon hearing God's promise, David was overwhelmed by the Lord's graciousness and declared, "Who am I, O Lord God? And what is my house that You have brought me this far? And yet this was a small thing in Your sight, O Lord God; and You have also spoken of Your servant's house for a great while to come… And now, O Lord God, You are God, and Your words are true, and You have promised this goodness to Your servant."[85] Interestingly, it is of note that the fall into moral ruin of many great leaders often occurs following closely behind some of their greatest successes.

It is so very natural to condemn others for the very injustices from which we excuse ourselves.

We can only imagine how nervous Nathan was about having to confront his friend and king with a message of repentance, knowing that nearly a year earlier David executed Uriah to prevent him from uncovering the king's infidelity. On God's appointed day, Nathan, in obedience, went to the king and told him a story of a situation that ended up being very similar to David's offense. As it is so very natural to condemn others for the very injustices from which we excuse ourselves, David's emotions surged with righteous indignation, demanding a harsh judgment for the cold-hearted man in Nathan's story. However, this was followed by Nathan's emphatic declaration, "You are the

84 2 Samuel 7.

85 2 Samuel 7:18-19, 28 (NKJV).

man!"[86] Fortunately, the Spirit's conviction led David to a place of acknowledgment of his sin which averted further disaster, though the consequences of his immorality would have lifelong ramifications.

I am astounded within this Biblical narrative to further learn of the depth of God's redeeming grace. The Lord is faithful to work through the most horrendous situations to reconcile and to restore for His ultimate glory. Nathan took the risk of confronting his king, encouraging him to return to God's purposes by speaking the truth in love. In time, David had four more children through his marriage to Bathsheba. The youngest, Solomon, would eventually be his heir and God's chosen son through whom David's ancestry would continue within the paternal lineage leading to Jesus Christ.[87] Yet tucked away in an obscure list of names in 1 Chronicles we learn of another of David and Bathsheba's children who also had a significant role in God's eternal plans. People often give great thought to the names that they give to their children. And occasionally, we name our kids after significant friends or family members who are dear to our heart. (I would assume my parents were fond of Disneyland.) David's third son from his relationship with Bathsheba was most likely named after the man who risked it all to confront his friend's transgression—Nathan.[88] What amazing grace God displays, as it was

86 2 Samuel 12:7 (NKJV).

87 Through Solomon would be the earthly lineage leading to Joseph, Jesus Christ's earthly father as noted in Matthew 1:6. However, Joseph was in the lineage of Coniah, son of Jehoiakim and Jeremiah 22:30 declared, "None of his descendants shall prosper, sitting on the throne of David, and ruling anymore in Judah," thus negating Joseph's paternal fulfillment of the prophesy of 2 Samuel 7. Of course, it is the divine intervention of Jesus' heavenly Father who enabled the prophecies to be rightly fulfilled without compromising the intricacies of God's word.

88 1 Chronicles 3:5; 2 Samuel 5:14.

through this son, Nathan, that King David's descendants find another link to the Messiah. As noted earlier, it was through Solomon that the Gospel of Matthew follows the lineage through Joseph to Jesus Christ. But in the Gospel of Luke we are given a script from heaven to learn that the mother of Jesus Christ, Mary, traces her roots back to Nathan. What an astounding plan, and what a gracious God we have! Despite his error, it was through David's failure that God would carry out His glorious design for redemption. And it is sometimes through our most devastating catastrophes that the Lord reveals His most wonderful love.

Be honest with yourself: are you a couple of degrees off from where God would have you be?

Perhaps you are in a season of life where you sense that the Holy Spirit is affording you the opportunity to take an azimuth check. These times come when there is unrest deep down in your heart, an apparent prompting from within; the subtle conviction arises and we can hear God's voice gently pricking our conscience. Questions may surface around some of our current relationships, actions, attitudes, thoughts, or even motives. Are there areas in your life that are leaking, possibly underneath the surface where no one around you can see? Be honest with yourself: are you a couple of degrees off from where God would have you be? Or even worse, are you 180 degrees off course and thus being confronted with your rebellion? Repent, turn around, and begin the journey of grace back to the loving arms of your heavenly Father. Let David's cry be your prayer of reconciliation:

"Have mercy on me, O God,
  according to Your steadfast love;
according to Your abundant mercy
  blot out my transgressions.
Wash me thoroughly from my iniquity,
  and cleanse me from my sin!
For I know my transgressions,
  and my sin is ever before me.
Against You, You only, have I sinned
  and done what is evil in Your sight,
so that You may be justified in Your words
  and blameless in Your judgment.

Create in me a clean heart, O God,
  and renew a right spirit within me.
Cast me not away from your presence,
  and take not your Holy Spirit from me.
Restore to me the joy of Your salvation,
  and uphold me with a willing spirit."[89]

If this is your situation, and there is a growing conviction that you need to make some crucial decisions to recalibrate your course, don't put this off another minute. The following suggestions and challenges will be important action steps for you to engage in immediately. Involve a respected friend, mentor, accountability partner, or pastor to assist in these vital commitments. When you are in a state of duress, you will often find benefit in getting things off your chest

89 Psalm 51:1-4, 10-12 (ESV).

by talking it out. In fact, most therapy models are based on this special need, so much so, that researchers often refer to talking things out as "cathartic ventilation." What is essential, however, is making sure the supportive friend or mentor provides a Godly sounding board and will speak the truth in love. In this way, your cathartic ventilation will avoid being simply a bunch of hot air.

Holding on Tight: Things to Consider

GROWING IN GRACE: The azimuth check to align one's life with Jesus Christ is clearly presented in the book of Romans in the Bible. Prayerfully read through the following verses and acknowledge each truth as you ask God to grow your relationship with Him. These verses are a pathway for personal transformation through the Scriptures:

- "There is none righteous, no, not one; there is none who understands; there is none who seeks after God. They have all turned aside; they have together become unprofitable; there is none who does good, no, not even one... for all have sinned and fall short of the glory of God."[90] - All people have sinned and come up short in being right with God.
- "For the wages of sin is death, but the free gift of God is eternal life in Christ Jesus our Lord."[91] - Sin leads to

90 Romans 3:10-12, 23 (NKJV).

91 Romans 6:23 (ESV).

eternal separation from God, but God provides eternal life in Christ Jesus.

- "But God shows His love for us in that while we were still sinners, Christ died for us."[92] - God so loved us that He provided His Son to die for our sins.
- "If you confess with your mouth the Lord Jesus and believe in your heart that God has raised Him from the dead, you will be saved... For 'whoever calls on the name of the LORD shall be saved.'"[93] - We receive salvation and eternal life by God's grace through the means of faith and repentance in Jesus Christ.
- "Therefore, having been justified by faith, we have peace with God through our Lord Jesus Christ, through whom also we have access by faith into this grace in which we stand, and rejoice in hope of the glory of God. Salvation through Jesus Christ brings us into a relationship of peace with God."[94]
- "Therefore, I urge you, brothers and sisters, in view of God's mercy, to offer your bodies as a living sacrifice, holy and pleasing to God–this is your true and proper worship. Do not conform to the pattern of this world, but be transformed by the renewing of your mind. Then you will be able to test and approve what God's will is–His good, pleasing and perfect will."[95] - Salvation will lead to the transformation of your life through the work of God's grace.

---

92 Romans 5:8 (ESV).

93 Romans 10:9, 13 (NKJV).

94 Romans 5:1-2 (NKJV).

95 Romans12:1-3 (NIV).

PRACTICAL CONSIDERATIONS: To avoid the sinkhole syndrome, consider the following encouragements that contribute to an ordered life:

- Become a committed member in a Bible teaching church.
- Get involved with a small group in your community that meets together as part of your church's community outreach.
- Be active in fulfilling God's calling and purpose in your life.
- Be intentional in sharing your faith with others in a way that affirms the love of God.
- Seek to be sensitive to God's leading through His Holy Spirit.
- Develop a growing commitment to live a life of integrity in your daily lifestyle and decisions.
- Know your limitations and weaknesses and seek for mentors who will hold you accountable and encourage your growth.
- Be a faithful steward of your time, talent and resources that demonstrates your God-honoring priorities.
- Spend time in prayer and the Scriptures every day as God's grace enables you to experience His voice and His presence.
- Seek for a balance in your personal, family, social, ministry, and career priorities.

CHAPTER FIVE

Believing in Dog

A number of years ago my youngest daughter introduced me to a light-hearted little book entitled *Cat & Dog Theology*. The premise of this book identifies various ways people view God as portrayed through our family pets. A dog says, "You pet me, you feed me, you shelter me, you love me, *You* must be God." A cat says, "You pet me, you feed me, you shelter me, you love me, *I* must be god."[96] Surely these animal traits give us a playful look into one of the fundamental tests to one's worldview. Who is on the throne of your life? In a sense, this question takes us to the dawning of human existence and to the initiation of human suffering.

At the core of Biblical faith is the ultimate truth that there is only one true God—and that one true God is not

96 Sjogren, Bob and Robison, Gerald. (2003). *Cat & Dog Theology: Rethinking Our Relationship with Our Master.* Authentic Media Publishing. Milton Keynes, United Kingdom. p 5.

you (or me). We experience true freedom when we yield to God's control of our circumstances and destiny. In the very beginning, God created man and woman in His image and likeness.[97] Adam and Eve were living in complete harmony with their Creator as they experienced the fullness of life without pain, sorrow, or death. Eventually a discourse was initiated by Satan which quickly led to the demise of their serenity. "For God knows that in the day you eat of it your eyes will be opened, and you will be like God, knowing good and evil."[98] Satan deviously twisted the truth that Adam and Eve were already *like* God as is clearly asserted in Genesis 1. Essential to the devil's temptation was his whisper to deceive them into thinking they could ultimately *be* God. From Genesis 3 to Revelation 22, the Bible reveals God's reconciliation, His bringing us back to our original state as He seeks to transform the people of faith into the image and likeness of Jesus Christ.[99] This reminds me of the title of a classic book written by Scottish theologian Henry Scougal (1650-1678), *The Life of God in the Soul of Man.* Astutely, Scougal's title encompasses a summary of

Christianity in its most essential core can be defined as the life of God in the human soul.

97 Genesis 1:26-27.

98 Genesis 3:5 (NKJV).

99 The substance of Biblical history is about God redeeming and reconciling things back to His original plan and design as affirmed by the following samples of Scripture: "But we all, with unveiled face, beholding as in a mirror the glory of the Lord, are being transformed into the same image from glory to glory, just as by the Spirit of the Lord" (2 Corinthians 3:18 NKJV). "For our citizenship is in heaven, from which we also eagerly wait for the Savior, the Lord Jesus Christ, who will transform our lowly body that it may be conformed to His glorious body, according to the working by which He is able even to subdue all things to Himself" (Philippians 3:20-21 NKJV). "And we know that all things work together for good to those who love God, to those who are the called according to His purpose. For whom He foreknew, He also predestined to be conformed to the image of His Son, that He might be the firstborn among many brethren" (Romans 8:28-29 NKJV). "And do not be conformed to this world, but be transformed by the renewing of your mind, that you may prove what is that good and acceptable and perfect will of God" (Romans 12:2 NKJV).

the ultimate meaning of life. Simply stated, Christianity in its most essential core can be defined as the life of God in the human soul. For God's life to be the life of our soul, it means that we need to let go of seeking to be the god of our life.

Along this theme of letting go, I have been enriched by the brief collection of letters found within the little book, *Let Go,* by Francois Fenelon (1651-1715). He was a very reflective and devout man who had a spiritual influence on many people in the Court of Louis the XIV during the 17th Century. Fenelon wrote in his twenty-eighth letter,

> "Please understand about love. I am not asking from you a love which is tender and emotional. All I ask is that your will should lean towards love, that you should make up your mind to love God, regardless of your feelings. And no matter what corrupt desires you should find in your heart, if you will make a decision to love God more than self and the whole world, He will be pleased."[100]

The idea that love is more than emotion is supported by Paul's familiar challenge in 1 Corinthians 13, which describes all the amazing virtues of love as active verbs, not as adjectives. Love is what we *do*, not just what we feel or say. As the title of Bob Goff's inspiring book affirms, *Love Does.* In harmony with this concept is the leadership book, *Love Works,* by Joel Manby. And we would do well to learn

100 Fenelon, Francois. (1973) *Let Go.* Whitaker House: New Kensington, PA. p. 58.

The 5 Love Languages (Gary Chapman) as we seek to be a blessing in our relationships. It is *Crazy Love* (Francis Chan) that inspires us to be aggressive in our bold compassion. These books about love have sold millions. It would appear that there is a longing in all of our hearts to be active in both giving and receiving love in its most authentic form. It is by our love for one another that the whole world should know that we belong to Jesus and that we reflect His nature.[101] It seems so simple, and yet people tend to make this truth so very complex.

Love is what we *do*, not just what we feel or say.

Life itself is not so simple, and neither is the consideration of eternity or contemplating the Divine; nor is pondering the great concepts of the Trinity, predestination and human will, the Scriptures' divine origin through fallible human beings; or better yet, understanding the dynamics among infralapsarianism, supralapsarianism and sublapsarianism. We just have to appreciate how theologians tend to pontificate the profundities of their prodigious cognitive proficiencies—or easier said, that smart people use a lot of big words. Perhaps this was Paul's motive in reminding us to keep things simple when he abridged his message to focus on the love displayed by the cross of Jesus Christ (cf. 1 Corinthians 2:2-4).

Steve Jobs' maxim was that, "simplicity is the ultimate sophistication." This idea was the driver toward refining the complexity of technology to produce the simplicity

101 John 13:35.

of the iPhone. The intricacies of Microelectromechanical Systems (MEMS) and the development of teeny tiny systems is downright fascinating. Inside an iPhone are over a hundred thousand proximity sensors, motion sensors, light sensors and moisture sensors. In addition, there are very complex binary codes and circuitry. All of these sensors work in harmony in order for us to have the simplest of devices that even a three year-old can operate with the touch of a finger. Perhaps it is with a chuckle that Jesus quipped in Matthew 18:3, "Assuredly, I say to you, unless you are converted and become as little children, you will by no means enter the kingdom of heaven." In all seriousness, life's complications are very real, but within the faith of the Gospel, God has simplified all of the mysteries of life and eternity into a succinct statement:

> "Little children, I shall be with you a little while longer. You will seek Me; and as I said to the Jews, 'Where I am going, you cannot come,' so now I say to you. A new commandment I give to you, that you love one another; as I have loved you, that you also love one another. By this all will know that you are My disciples, if you have love for one another."[102]

Notice that Jesus refers to His disciples as "little children." Like the touch of a finger on the pulse of life, the convolutions of existence are reduced to the simplicity of

102 John 13:33-35 (NKJV).

LOVE. Personally, I believe we would do well if we follow Fenelon's wisdom in even the hardest of circumstances to "lean towards love." If there's potential conflict, die to yourself and engage love. If there's an undesirable task or chore at hand, *Love Does.* If there is a need to be met, have *Crazy Love.* Why? Because *Love Works,* and because it's His Eternal *Love Language.*

I am reminded throughout the Scriptures that God's ways are eternally beyond what we can logically figure out or even imagine. In fact, the prophet of Isaiah had a vision of God seated on His throne and he cried out in repentance and worship, "Woe is me, for I am undone!"[103] Later in his ministry God revealed to Isaiah, "'For My thoughts are not your thoughts, nor are your ways My ways,' says the Lord. For as the heavens are higher than the earth, so are My ways higher than your ways, and My thoughts than your thoughts.'"[104] Frankly, there are a lot of things about God's providence that don't make sense to me, but then again, only the cat's worldview demands dominion of reason. When I read through the Bible, it is odd to me that of all the people God could have chosen to save amongst the idolaters of Jericho, He thought Rahab the prostitute was a good pick. Not only that, but He also chose to place her within the ancestry of Jesus Christ.[105] I won't get into the reasoning behind Isaiah's naked prophecies[106] or Ezekiel's culinary expertise of cooking over cow dung while lying on

103 Isaiah 6:5 (NKJV).

104 Isaiah 55:8-9 (NKJV).

105 Ruth 4:18-22; Matthew 1:5.

106 Isaiah 20:2-3.

his side for 430 days.[107] God's commentary was needed to guide Samuel when he was instructed to anoint the unlikely young candidate, David, the son of Jesse, to be the future king of Israel: "For the Lord does not see as man sees; for man looks at the outward appearance but the Lord looks at the heart."[108] One of the greatest of all theologians, Paul the Apostle, had, perhaps a hint for us in his letter to the Romans about justification by faith. At the close of eleven chapters where he discusses the remarkable revelation of God's love and grace in relation to our sin, Paul concludes with the exclamation,

> "Oh, the depth of the riches and wisdom and knowledge of God! How unsearchable are His judgments and how inscrutable His ways! 'For who has known the mind of the Lord, or who has been His counselor? Or who has given a gift to him that he might be repaid?' For from Him and through Him and to Him are all things. To Him be glory forever. Amen."[109]

I get the sense that after writing about the wonder of God's grace in salvation, Paul was humbled and brought to the realization that God's ways eternally exceed our understanding. Like Isaiah, Paul was overcome with praise in the contemplation of the divine ways of God. What an error for people to fall into the place where they believe

---

107 Ezekiel 4:4-17.

108 1 Samuel 16:7 (NKJV).

109 Romans 11:33-36 (ESV).

that their finite, limited perspective is central in determining their purpose or destiny apart from the wisdom of God. It is right for God to put us in our place when we become full of ourselves and focused on ourselves, as it is His intention to free us *from* ourselves. Such prudence, the Lord declared through the psalmist, Asaph, when he wrote the lyrics, "These things you have done, and I kept silent; you thought that I was altogether like you; but I will rebuke you, and set them in order before your eyes."[110] How tragic to hold to the position to think that God is in *my* image, rather that I am created in *His* image.

How tragic to hold to the position to think that God is in *my* image, rather that I am created in *His* image.

I am reminded of an ancient Asian parable about an old farmer and his son. The poor farmer had worked his fields for many years but was quite poor. Each day a neighbor would visit to see how things were progressing through his hardships. One day his horse ran away. Upon hearing the news, his neighbor passed by and acknowledged the bad luck. "How do you know it's bad?" came the reply from the old man. The next morning the horse returned, bringing with it three other wild horses. "How wonderful!" the neighbor exclaimed. "How do you know it's wonderful?" replied the farmer. The following day, his son tried to ride one of the untamed horses, and he was thrown off only to break his leg in several places. The neighbor came again to offer his sympathy on the poor farmer's misfortune. "How

110 Psalm 50:21 (ESV).

do you know this is a misfortune?" came the response. The day after, the military came through the village and drafted all of the young men to go to war. Seeing the young man in bed with a broken leg, they excused him from his service. The neighbor congratulated the farmer on how well things had turned out. "How do you know?" said the wise father. Thereafter, the soldiers returned with great wealth from their military spoils. All the families of the village were rich, except the poor farmer whose son was still injured, as he didn't go off to war. "Oh, what a pity," observed the neighbor on his next visit. "How do you know we are at a loss?" came the response. As it turned out, another army had heard of the great wealth in the village and they assaulted the village that night, killing most of the men. However, they spared the farmer and his son, as they were still quite poor.

How do we really know what foresight God has about our difficult or fortunate circumstances, given the glory of God's wisdom? A dear friend of ours, Courtney, was a struggling make-up artist in Hollywood. While parallel parking in Los Angeles, she accidentally grazed an expensive brand new Range Rover. The two drivers exchanged information and Courtney recalled thinking that she wished she had met the owner of the Range Rover under different circumstances, as she seemed to be such a nice person. It wasn't until she returned home that Courtney looked at the information and immediately recognized her name. The Range Rover was driven by one of Hollywood's well-known make-up specialists. Eventually a follow up call was made and through the conversation a friendship was kindled. In fact, the gracious new acquaintance invited our friend to a networking opportunity to expand her clientele. Was the car accident bad? Was the invite good? How do you know? Similarly, my wife recently received a prayer request from a couple that were in a life-threatening car accident. The driver was rushed into surgery to mend a compound fracture, wherein it was discovered that he had a previously undetected heart problem. If this anomaly had been left unattended much longer, it would have resulted in his death. The accident ended up saving his life. How do you know? God knows!

This quandary of dubious providence became very poignant to me as a result of an intervention that I was asked to lead for an emergency response casualty. There was a very dramatic 911 call as a result of a pool drowning of a three year-old who had been left unattended for about twenty minutes at a large family gathering. The child did not survive, and due to the heartbreaking nature of the situation, the incident commander believed the crews would benefit from an official critical incident stress debriefing. This is a formal process that takes a couple of hours where the involved rescue personnel are allowed to vent their thoughts and experiences. The process for these responders proved to be very beneficial and at the close of our time together I asked each of the participants to estimate how many drowning accidents they had responded to within their careers. Sadly, this was not a rare experience in Southern California given the number of pools in our communities. However, one of the seasoned captains reminded all of us of the many children's lives that have been saved through their efforts. A number of the medics started to share some of those experiences, which brought a sense of great hope and satisfaction for what they do. As an addendum, the captain went on to narrate an amazing testimony of a rescue that happened earlier in his career.

A couple had left their two-and-a-half-year-old with a teenage babysitter while they went out for a Saturday lunch date. Soon after the parents left, the little guy was put in his bed for a nap. Shortly thereafter the sitter was chatting on her phone in the living room with one of her girlfriends. The call was eventually interrupted when the family dog was jumping and barking from outside the front screen door. The teen opened the door and the soaking-wet family dog ran through the house barking. The sitter tried to quiet the dog to avoid waking the child, and when she peeked in the child's room she was startled to find that he was not in his bed. The dog was now barking at the rear patio glass doors, through which the babysitter saw the child laying beside the pool. In a panic, she ran to the child who had been in the pool and the child was not breathing. The teen had the sense to immediately call 911, and fortunately the residence was close to a fire station. When the paramedics arrived they quickly revived the child who was transported to a local hospital for further evaluation. When completing the incident report, the paramedics inquired as to who pulled the child out of the pool, as they had noticed upon arrival that there was a wet trail on the pavement indicating that the child had been dragged to the spot where the resuscitation was done. From the testimony of the babysitter and the evidence of the wet canine, they surmised that the dog had actually rescued the child. I have since verified the accuracy of this report to counter those who may be skeptics. Within the providence of God this dog rescued the child, got the attention of the teenager, and probably would have called 911 if the sitter weren't already on the phone. And for those who have a hard time believing in God, at least they must believe in dog (especially if they are a little dyslexic)!

God's ways aren't always our ways and His thoughts aren't always aligned with our thoughts. The other day I sent a quick email where I meant to sign off saying, "Have a *good* day," but instead I accidentally left off an "o" and typed, "Have a *god* day." That little error reminded me that every day should be a *God day* as we learn to *let go* and *let God.* I have come to realize that when I just don't know what to think about a situation, I need to fall back on what I do know—that God is awesome![111] If you find yourself in a time of great uncertainty and questions are racing in your mind that are causing you to doubt God's promises, your current life situation, or simply life itself, on your next day off take some focused time to rest, reflect, and gain

111 If one ever questions the ways of God, it is very beneficial to remember what Scripture reveals about the nature of God. "The Lord, the Lord, a God merciful and gracious, slow to anger, and abounding in steadfast love and faithfulness, keeping steadfast love for thousands, forgiving iniquity and transgression and sin" (Exodus 34:6-7 ESV). "The Lord is slow to anger and abounding in steadfast love, forgiving iniquity and transgression" (Numbers 14:18 ESV). "But you, O Lord, are a God merciful and gracious, slow to anger and abounding in steadfast love and faithfulness" (Psalm 86:16 ESV). "The Lord works righteousness and justice for all who are oppressed. The Lord is merciful and gracious, slow to anger and abounding in steadfast love" (Psalm 103:6, 8 ESV). "The Lord is gracious and merciful, slow to anger and abounding in steadfast love. The Lord is good to all, and his mercy is over all that he has made" (Psalm 145:8-9 ESV). "But you are a God ready to forgive, gracious and merciful, slow to anger and abounding in steadfast love, and did not forsake them" (Nehemiah 9:17 ESV). "For I knew that you are a gracious God and merciful, slow to anger and abounding in steadfast love, and relenting from disaster" (Jonah 4:2 ESV). "Who is a God like you, pardoning iniquity and passing over transgression for the remnant of his inheritance? He does not retain his anger forever, because he delights in steadfast love. He will again have compassion on us; he will tread our iniquities underfoot. You will cast all our sins into the depths of the sea" (Micah 7:18-19 ESV). No matter what our circumstances may appear to be, always recall that "God is love" (1 John 4:8 ESV).

perspective. Get away from all the hustle and bustle of life and slow down enough to really consider the suggestions below.

Holding on Tight: Things to Consider

GROWING IN GRACE: In times when we just don't know, we need to fall back on what we do know. And according to the Scriptures, we know that God is gracious, merciful and kind. Consider the following verses if you ever doubt the faithfulness and goodness of God:

- "And the LORD passed before him and proclaimed, 'The Lord, the Lord God, merciful and gracious, longsuffering, and abounding in goodness and truth, keeping mercy for thousands, forgiving iniquity and transgression and sin.'"[112]
- "The LORD is longsuffering and abundant in mercy, forgiving iniquity and transgression."[113]
- "Therefore know that the LORD your God, He *is* God, the faithful God who keeps covenant and mercy for a thousand generations with those who love Him and keep His commandments."[114]

112 Exodus 34:6-7 (NKJV).

113 Numbers 14:18 (NKJV).

114 Deuteronomy 7:9 (NKJV).

- "But You *are* God, ready to pardon, gracious and merciful, slow to anger, abundant in kindness, and did not forsake them."[115]
- "But You, O Lord, *are* a God full of compassion, and gracious, longsuffering and abundant in mercy and truth."[116]
- "Return to the LORD your God, for He *is* gracious and merciful, slow to anger, and of great kindness; and He relents from doing harm."[117]
- Who *is* a God like You, pardoning iniquity and passing over the transgression of the remnant of His heritage? He does not retain His anger forever, because He delights *in* mercy. He will again have compassion on us, and will subdue our iniquities. You will cast all our sins into the depths of the sea."[118]
- "Beloved, let us love one another, for love is of God; and everyone who loves is born of God and knows God. He who does not love does not know God, for God is love."[119]
- "And this is the testimony: that God has given us eternal life, and this life is in His Son. He who has the Son has life; he who does not have the Son of God does not have life. These things I have written to you who believe in the name of the Son of God, that you may

115 Nehemiah 9:17 (NKJV).

116 Psalm 86:15 (NKJV).

117 Joel 2:13 (NKJV).

118 Micah 7:18-19 (NKJV).

119 1 John 4:7-8 (NKJV).

know that you have eternal life, and that you may *continue to* believe in the name of the Son of God."[120]

PRACTICAL CONSIDERATIONS: When facing a devastating hardship or difficulty, sometimes we need time for the journey to recovery to bring healing. Have grace for yourself and for others as you make space for a season of adjustment. The following suggestions can be helpful in navigating towards a future of hope:

- Promote activities that foster strong social support. Nurture old and new friendships.
- Seek for strong role models who can serve as mentors.
- Engage in regular physical exercise.
- Follow a moral compass that aligns with a legacy of noble character.
- Practice optimism and look for the good in the Lord, His people and His providence.
- Seek guidance and counsel in actively dealing with your current challenges.
- Be open minded and flexible in the way you are thinking about your situation. Avoid being overly rigid and dogmatic in your perspective.

120 1 John 5:11-13 (NKJV).

CHAPTER SIX

No Regrets

I have served a lot of people who have found themselves in a time of major life adjustment. These moments come within seasons of great merriment or at periods of deep loss. These are the times that cause us to pause, to reflect once again about the more lofty things of life. Whether at a wedding or a special family celebration, or during a time of sickness or calamity, we are afforded the opportunity to evaluate our life's purpose. Some of us want time to stand still to discover and appreciate the joys of the moment. Others are longing for the days to hurry by, hoping the burdens of the present will be dissolved in a new season. I'm reminded of A.W. Tozer's wisdom:

> "How completely satisfying to turn from our limitations to a God who has none. Eternal years lie in His heart. For Him time does not pass, it remains;

> and those who are in Christ share with Him all the riches of limitless time and endless years. God never hurries. There are no deadlines against which He must work. Only to know this is to quiet our spirits and relax our nerves. For those out of Christ, time is a devouring beast." [121]

The life of God in our very souls is to be savored each tick of the day.

Every year, every month, every day, every hour, every minute is given to us as a precious gift, all within the bounds of God's eternal perspective. To us is given the privilege of being stewards of this most precious gift—TIME. We can invest time, enjoy time, and savor time as we journey through life's experiences. Yet sadly, many simply spend time, waste time, squander time, or just try to get through each day's problems, inevitably missing out on precious gifts that God has for us each moment. People rush through life, and like Peter in the Bible, they "follow Him at a distance."[122] And then, finally, life slaps us on the side of the head and there's an awakening of regrets, having missed the extravagance of God's timeless presence. Unfortunately, people often make unwise choices when they are not mindful of the long-term consequences of their decisions. The life of God in our very souls is to be savored each tick of the day. He bids us to drink of this life throughout every waking hour. To defy His principles will almost certainly lead to a life of misgivings and missed

121 Tozer, A.W. (1961). *The Knowledge of the Holy.* HarperCollins Publishers, New York, NY p. 47.

122 Matthew 26:58 (NKJV).

blessings. To live daily within the awareness of God's precepts and presence provides the foundation of a life of no regrets.

Jesus said, "If you abide in Me, and My words abide in you, you will ask what you desire, and it shall be done for you. By this My Father is glorified, that you bear much fruit; so you will be My disciples."[123] *Abiding*. The gracious experience of abiding is a subtle, yet profound, concept of faith that will bring a constant fragrance to your heart. I believe that if you take time to really appreciate this practice, it will alleviate many of the lesser ills that plague the soul through the "lust of the flesh, the lust of the eyes, and the pride of life."[124] Abiding is mentioned ten times in ten verses in John 15. In abiding, spiritual fruit multiplies, prayers are answered, God is glorified, and the heart is calmed. In its essence, abiding is the hope of grace. The word "abide" in Greek is *meno,* which means, "to stay, remain, live, dwell, lodge."[125] The encouragement is to stay connected to the Source of our life—Jesus Christ.

It has always been my passion that my kids would find their foundation and purpose in life in being Christ-centered.

As a father, it has always been my passion that my kids would find their foundation and purpose in life in being Christ-centered. I've continuously prayed that my children would grow more and more in love with Jesus to avoid the pitfalls of empty religion. Through the years I

---

123 John 15:7-8 (NKJV).

124 1 John 2:16 (NKJV).

125 Bauer, Walter. (1957). *A Greek-English Lexicon of the New Testament and Other Early Christian Literature.* Chicago Press, Chicago, IL. p. 503.

have encouraged them to be active in their church, serving God's Kingdom, sharing their faith, and growing within the means of grace. I have also sought to guard them from falling into the routines of obligatory religion, empty works, and guilt-ridden duties of legalism. But on the other hand, I've cautioned them not to grow idle in grace, not to settle into the comfortable place of being a spectator of Christ's work, watching from afar, and never engaging fully in God's calling for their lives. God beckons us to be a light and witness to Him and to the people Jesus brings before us every day. To ignore the Great Commission and the Great Commandment[126] is to ignore Jesus' passion. When we live within God's purposes, the benefit of the abiding life will overflow into all that we are and all that we do. When we find ourselves overly busy with the routines of life, we will slowly grow dry and parched, bearing a harvest of discontent, conflict, dissatisfaction, and bitter-tasting fruit. Still worse, if we yoke our heart with the burdens of religious rituals and traditions we will remove *Christ* right out of *Christ*ianity. Abiding in Jesus is the fulcrum that lets our spirits flourish and escape many other perils.

God longs for us to discover Him in the ordinary, and even in the mundane.

Pause for a moment before reading on and ask God to speak to your heart. Are you in an abiding relationship with Jesus Christ? Are you experiencing the richness of the faith that He has for you? Are you abounding in the fruit

126 Matthew 28:19-20 and Matthew 22:36-40.

of a rich faith that is saturated in the things of the Holy Spirit? Are you passionate about Jesus? God longs for us to discover Him in the ordinary, and even in the mundane. He waits for us to commune with Him in the everyday, common routines of life. Transformation takes place as our minds are renewed within God's abiding presence, even when discomforts abound. "I beseech you therefore, brethren, by the mercies of God, that you present your bodies a living sacrifice, holy, acceptable to God, which is your reasonable service. And do not be conformed to this world, but be transformed by the renewing of your mind, that you may prove what is that good and acceptable and perfect will of God."[127]

All of this brings me to the delight of the beautiful concept of the *quotidian.* The word itself simply means "daily, commonplace, ordinary."[128] It is a concept that describes probably eighty percent of our human existence within our regular, ordinary routines. However, when sparked by the majesty of Christ, our daily routines can ignite into a flame of passion and purpose. (I'm borrowing some metaphors from Kathleen Norris' book, *The Quotidian Mysteries.*)[129] But think for a moment about the mundane chores of housecare—sweeping, vacuuming, cleaning, gardening, polishing, and dusting *ad infinitum.*[130] Most of us are a bit allergic to emptying the dishwasher or leaning over the sink to wash the dinner dishes. But on the other hand,

---

127 Romans 12:1-2 (NKJV).

128 Merriam-Webster. (1995). *Webster's New American Dictionary.* Smithmark Publishers, New York: NY, p. 427.

129 Norris, Kathleen. (1998). *The Quotidian Mysteries: Laundry, Liturgy and "Women's Work,"* Paulist Press: New York, NY.

130 *Ad infinitum* is a Latin phrase meaning "to infinity." Or we could borrow a definition from that contemporary sage in *Toy Story*, Buzz Lightyear: "To infinity and beyond!"

if you watch children play at these very same tasks, you get a glimpse into the delights of life. Fill the sink with soapsuds, cups, plates, and bowls, and they will enjoy the task at hand. The quotidian things of life can become the temple of holy leisure as God invites us to play and experience His presence as we soak in His love and hear His whispers. These experiences become our manna of the day, our daily bread. It is only good for the moment, as tomorrow it will spoil. In writing about manna in the Old Testament, Moses recorded, "So when they measured it by omers, he who gathered much had nothing left over, and he who gathered little had not lack. Every man had gathered according to each one's need. And Moses said, 'Let no one leave any of it till morning.'"[131] In a similar way, God bids us to walk with Him throughout each day's experiences, gleaning from the orchards of the ordinary as they blossom the soul. Sadly while wandering in the wilderness, God's people eventually took the daily provision of manna for granted. Similarly, we too can miss the Lord's nourishment amongst the quotidian moments and hassles of each day.

My encouragement is to discover that childlike faith of savoring each day's routines as an opportunity to experience God's joys. Don't miss His playful voice amongst the deafening sound of life's clutter. Stay connected to the Vine throughout each day's mundane experiences, and what is ordinary will be transformed into the extraordinary. And when I'm old and wrinkled all over, and you see me sitting alone, overcome with a smile and a chuckle, know

131 Exodus 16:18-19 (NKJV).

this: I'm just enjoying God's voice and drinking in the pleasure of the moment as I play in the suds of the quotidian.

As I share these concepts, I know they can be filtered through the stories of those who are brokenhearted, depressed, wounded, scarred, and full of regrets. We must be reminded of the fact that our life's fulfillment is not about our life's accomplishments. Our salvation and calling are not about our works of righteousness but "according to God's own purpose and grace, which was given to us in Christ Jesus before time began."[132] The Apostle Paul brought this same perspective in his encouragement to Titus when he confirmed, "In hope of eternal life which God, who cannot lie, promised before time began."[133] Think of this: before time began, before there were any successive moments, God had *you* on His mind. Thus *before* time, God created the gift of time, so that we could experience His love through the filling of His Spirit *within* time. Be challenged to relentlessly draw close to the Lord, empowered by His grace every year, month, day, hour, and moment. Don't squander the moments, but rather, live every day mindful that you can choose to obey God's plans and purposes, within which you will never have regrets. "You will show me the path of life; in Your presence *is* fullness of joy; at Your right hand are pleasures forevermore."[134] Glorify God and enjoy Him forever and ever and ever and ever and ever.

---

132 2 Timothy 1:9 (NKJV).

133 Titus 1:2 (NKJV). Also note Paul's encouragement, "just as He chose us in Him before the foundation of the world, that we should be holy and without blame before Him in love" (Ephesians 1:4 NKJV). "According to the revelation of the mystery kept secret since the world began" (Romans 16:25 NKJV).

134 Psalm 16:11 (NKJV).

As a chaplain, I often serve people towards the end of their life when their remaining moments are at a minimum. It is common for individuals in this stage of life to look back at missed opportunities and broken relationships. It is during the sunset years of life that a person's regrets can begin to weigh heavy on the heart. Such was the discovery by Wendy Lustbader in her book entitled *What's Worth Knowing*. Wendy Lustbader was an affiliate assistant professor at the University of Washington. She was also a counselor at Seattle's Pike Market Medical Clinic. In her book she recorded reflections of more than one hundred of the most profound elders she had met through her work. We can gain such wisdom from hearing the reflections of those who are in the final months of their lives. For example, Jerry Kliman at age eighty-two reminisced, "When I married Sara in 1942, I thought she was the most beautiful woman in the world. Every day of our life together, I have felt the same way.... My wife is my best friend and lifelong companion. Every time I look at her, I still feel like the luckiest man around."[135] Martin DeGeorge at age ninety-nine asserted, "What makes a good marriage? Hard work. We should know. Harriet and I have been working at it for over seventy-five years. Young couples today think it's a piece of cake. Then when it's rough, they give it up. Sure, there have been times I wanted to walk

We've had at least ten thousand misunderstandings, ten thousand hurts, and another ten thousand apologies.

135 Lustbader, Wendy. (2001) *What's Worth Knowing*. Penguin Publishing Group. New York, NY. p.94.

out and never look back. Now I have to help her to the bathroom. You think that's fun? Half the time, we don't even get there in time. But she's still my sweet bride. We've had at least ten thousand misunderstandings, ten thousand hurts, and another ten thousand apologies."[136] What amazing insights we can glean from those who are forging ahead of us on life's journey. Whether it is the wisdom of regrets to avoid or the ethics that add value to our relationships, we would be wise to heed the experience of our elders.

I frequently ask seasoned married couples about the key principles that have enhanced their relationship. At an American Red Cross banquet I once attended, I had the honor of sitting next to a retired admiral and his wife who had been married for over sixty years. I popped the question: what was the secret of six decades of marital bliss? His wife quipped, "Well you know he was in the Navy, so he was gone a lot." That wasn't quite the answer I had expected, but indeed, it was probably their humorous reality. I once heard another elder husband challenge young women to hold out for a man that had two distinct benefits, "First, only marry a truly godly man, and second, marry an archaeologist." He added, "An archaeologist will always be attentive, since the older you get the more interest he will have in you." It is interesting that little girls often grow up to marry men just like their dads, and perhaps that's why so many moms cry at weddings.

It breaks my heart to witness so many people who live with crushing regrets about their families and marriages.

136 ibid p. 104

Their legacy is littered with broken promises, abandonment and self-centered pursuits, usually at the expense of shattered relationships and vain gratifications. Wendy Lustbader recorded one such distressing confession when Jerry Hersch (age seventy) admitted, "I was too good at keeping grudges. If somebody crossed me, that was it. Finished. You could get down on your knees and I wouldn't bat an eyelash. I dropped friends right and left. No one could live up to my standards. Then my daughter wrote me off. I didn't come through on a promise, and zap, she was done with me. She wouldn't let me explain. I got a taste of my own medicine. It's been more than twenty years now and we haven't said a word to each other. I've been wanting to call my daughter, but it's too late. I let too many years go by."[137] These thoughts Jerry shared on the day before his death from cancer. It is a lie to believe that God can't work His grace and redemption even at one's very end. The thief on the cross gives testimony that it is never too late.[138]

I must confess here that I also have a major regret in my life. In fact, I can recall the very day with great detail. It was a decision I made that I have to live with for the rest of my life. My children are all aware of my fiasco and as one might expect, it's embarrassing. It was a very poor choice I actually made on my wedding day. To this day, my wife says, "What were you thinking?" Though she gave me the freedom in my early days to fail, I still wish I could take that decision back. "If only… I should have… I wish I

137 Lustbader, Wendy. (2001) *What's Worth Knowing*. Penguin Publishing Group. New York, NY. p. 212.

138 See Luke 23:32-43.

didn't!... What if?" These exclamations and questions pour out of us all, because we have all done things in certain situations without thinking about the lifetime ramifications. It's when we bargain with ourselves, and at times with God, wishing we could somehow alter the past. My blunder, you ask? My major regret took place more than thirty-five years ago and I remember it as if it were yesterday. I wore a powder blue tuxedo with a ruffle shirt on my wedding day. Now there is dumb, there is dumber, and there is downright reckless. What *was* I thinking? Apparently, I was trying to avoid a quotidian moment. For sure, I wasn't thinking about making a fashion statement, and certainly not one that would outlive the early 1980s.

Frequently in my crisis intervention work, I am alongside of people that are wrecked by the horrible challenges that have come their way. As a common practice, when faced with difficulty, I encourage people to see their future with a mind's eye on the present. Looking five, ten, or even twenty years into the future, what do they want that future to look like? Faced with the decisions of today, people are encouraged to seek a future where hindsight would possess no regrets. And even if poor decisions or moral failure have been a part of your recent past, you still can choose a path that will bring restoration to avert the grief of remorse. It is never too late to pick up the phone and reconcile with those we have hurt or been hurt by. Moses said it well after reviewing the blessings and curses within God's law: " I call heaven and earth as witnesses today against you, that I have set before you life and death, blessing and cursing; therefore choose life, that both you and your descendants may live."[139] Based on our choices, what awaits us is either a legacy of divine destiny, or a disaster. My encouragement for you is to choose life and be blessed! And men, if you are indecisive about your clothing options for a special event, choose what your wife would pick. And if she isn't there, ask your daughters. If you are a single man, ask your sister or a trusted female acquaintance. And if there is absolutely no female wisdom available, maybe just stay home and have a bowl of ice cream—people never regret that.

Holding on Tight: Things to Consider

GROWING IN GRACE: All of us are uniquely designed in how we prefer to spend time with the Lord. In addition, there are certain experiences, practices, and environments where our faith is energized more dynamically.[140] In review of this brief list below, discuss with a friend or family member how you individually are best impacted for growth in your faith:

- Through nature and God's creation.
- Within your intellectual and theological pursuits of study and learning.
- In a social environment with family, friends, and/or mentors where you commune together in the things of God.

139 Deuteronomy 30:19 (NKJV).

140 For a great tool to assess your personal preferences in spiritual growth environments, see: Ortberg, John and Barton, Ruth Haley. (2001). *An Ordinary Day with Jesus: Participant's Guide.* Barrington, IL: Willow Creek Association, 2001), p. 67.

- Through service projects and activities where you give of yourself to assist others.
- In times of solitude and quiet contemplation.
- During times of worship, whether in a congregation or alone.
- In times of leisure doing activities you enjoy.

PRACTICAL CONSIDERATIONS: Though there are many practical suggestions to deal with our stresses in life, basically all of our options can be summarized within these four essential considerations. Evaluate your current stress load within these options:

- Remove yourself from the environment or situation of the stressor.
- Strengthen your coping resources to deal with and adapt to the stressor.
- Change how the stressor is personally viewed through a reappraisal of the experience.
- Do activities that provide a release or ventilation of the stressor experience.

CHAPTER SEVEN

What's in the Trunk?

On a beautiful spring day in San Diego, a family joined together on a hillside cemetery to pay respects to their great aunt who passed away in her late eighties. As the graveside service was about to begin, a quiet came upon the small gathering. People seemed to be drinking in the moment as a light breeze rustled the nearby trees and a flock of birds landed close by. The youngest in the group, at age four, was evaluating her surroundings as she gazed up and down between the grave and the coffin trying to make sense of this new experience. Just about the time when the pastor was going to open the service in prayer, the preschooler tugged on her mother's dress and loudly posed the most natural of questions, "Mommy, what's in the trunk?"

I have reflected on this question over the years, as her question will conjure up a vast array of memories that encompass a person's life testimony. One's life narrative includes many successes and failures, highs and lows, and innumerable joyful and painful episodes. The human life-cycle progresses through the epochs of spills, drills, frills, bills, ills, pills, and finally, wills. Some say there are four stages of life that are illustrated through the parody of Santa Claus' life: (1) When you *believe* in Santa Claus. (2) When you *don't believe* in Santa Claus. (3) When you *are* Santa Claus. (4) When you *look like* Santa Claus. I realized recently that I am now closer to that final stage when a co-worker's two-and-a half year-old daughter pointed at me from her stroller and exclaimed, "Look, Daddy, there's Noah!"

Our life's legacy is most notably defined by who we are in Jesus Christ.

Sadly, what's in the trunk is often merely summarized by the dash between the dates on a person's tombstone.[141] The question of the trunk should challenge all of us as to how we want our story to be written. What life narrative do you hope to leave to future generations? What are the virtues by which you want to be known and remembered? What is the epitaph of your time on earth that will echo beyond the grave? Our life's legacy is most notably defined by who we are in Jesus Christ. To receive Jesus Christ as our Lord and Savior will determine an eternal legacy that transcends all of the troubles of the moment.

When my first granddaughter was born it was one of those new segues in life that I experienced with much

141 See *The Dash* by Linda Ellis. *http://joyce.taron.net/the-dash-a-poem-by-linda-ellis*

reflection. The extended family lingered impatiently in the waiting room for a chance to meet Kennedy for the first time. Excited conversations were taking place throughout the room as we each waited for our opportunity to enter my daughter's room one-by-one; meanwhile, I strategically and successfully planted myself closest to the entrance to be the first to go into the room. When the occasion was provided for me to enter, it was one of those moments in life that will forever be sealed in my heart. My spirit was overwhelmed with God's love as I saw my daughter cuddling her precious baby, her smile lighting up the room.

"It's amazing how much you just love her, huh?" I asked.

Shiloh nodded in affirmation as tears welled up in her eyes.

"You never knew this kind of love existed before, did you?" was my next question.

Again my daughter nodded.

"It's the love your mother and I have always had for you, but we could never explain it to you until now. You can't know this love until you experience it for yourself."

And of course, the most natural question that a father could ask at this moment came next:

"Are you ready to have another one?"

And to my delight she affirmed, "Most definitely!"

What followed was one of those timeless revelations that further bonded both of our hearts with our heavenly Father. I hugged and kissed my daughter, and then was blessed to hold my granddaughter for the very first time. In that very instant, familiar verses flooded my mind, "For God so loved the world that He gave His only begotten

Son, that whoever believes in Him should not perish but have everlasting life. For God did not send His Son into the world to condemn the world, but that the world through Him might be saved."[142] "God shows his love for us in that while we were still sinners, Christ died for us."[143] We simply cannot begin to fathom the love that God has for us, in that He sacrificed His one and only Son that we might have His life. And this ransom was not made because we were lovable, but rather because God is love. Brimming with these surging contemplations, I couldn't help but to pose this unthinkable question to my daughter:

"Could you ever imagine sacrificing little Kennedy for the sins of another?"

It was ghastly to even imagine such a thought at that moment, but it is that love that conquered death and the grave for us. Through His inexhaustible grace we are saved through faith in Jesus Christ. Divine love enables our story to be redefined by the significance of God's ultimate glory in redemption. From the moment of one's conception, until the closing of the trunk, God is using all things to reveal His reality through His wondrous redemptive love.

We often entertain such extreme thoughts about God during eccentric times in life. It is during those oscillations between pleasure and agony that people are sometimes brought to the point of a "crisis of faith." It is the arena where we are challenged about what we believe about God, the nature of reality, and the essence of our worldview. It is there that faith is sometimes embraced or even transformed.

---

142 John 3:16-17 (NKJV).

143 Romans 5:8 (ESV).

At other times, people reject faith or allow for their faith to be distorted. For some, thoughts of God give birth to deep gratefulness and worship, while others feel abandoned by God, finding it hard to pray. Some even drift away from the integrity of righteousness, compromising the eternal for the temporal. In Jesus' parable of the sower, we are shown how spiritual attack, pleasure, and pain each carry the potential to corrupt and block the richness of God's purposes for our souls. But it is the soil of authentic faith that produces the fruit that God seeks within the heart that is surrendered to the Lord.[144]

As a young warrior and psalmist, David seemed to see things as black and white, with little room for gray.

Such was another of King David's experiences during a season of maltreatment under King Saul. In his youth, David dealt with injustice and false accusations in an attempt to vindicate his self-asserted righteousness. As a young warrior and psalmist, David seemed to see things as black and white, with little room for gray. His youthful zeal easily condemned the wickedness of others while exonerating his own virtues and strengths. In fact, under his youthful vigor we sense a hint of entitlement when he asserted, "The Lord rewarded me according to my righteousness; according to the cleanness of my hands He has recompensed me. For I have kept the ways of the Lord, and have not wickedly departed from my God."[145] Some seasons of life things go so well that we can wrongly conclude that we

---

144 Matthew 13:1-23

145 Psalm 18:20-21 (NKJV).

are being blessed because of our personal accomplishments. In contrast, it is often not until we come to grips with the greatness of God's grace in our failures and struggles that we discover it is only by *His* mercies that we are benefited in life. During the crushing times of injustice, the yielded heart is provided the opportunity to comprehend that it is God who is often behind our circumstances, intentionally yet tenderly seeking to humble our lofty perceptions. Years after his deep repentance, the king was forced to flee Jerusalem when faced with the painful betrayal of close friends and family. It was a mature David who refrained from trying to prove his personal innocence while he experienced injustices inflicted by others. It was by the God-given strength of humility and brokenness that David held his tongue and exalted God within his pain as he wrote:

> "I said, I will guard my ways,
> lest I sin with my tongue;
> I will restrain my mouth with a muzzle,
> while the wicked are before me.
> I was mute with silence,
> I held my peace even from good;
> and my sorrow was stirred up.
> My heart was hot within me;
> while I was musing, the fire burned.
> Then I spoke with my tongue:
>
> 'LORD, make me to know my end,
> and what is the measure of my days,
> that I may know how frail I am.

Indeed, You have made my days as handbreadths,
and my age is as nothing before You;
certainly every man at his best state is but vapor.'
Selah.

Surely every man walks about like a shadow;
surely they busy themselves in vain;
he heaps up riches,
and does not know who will gather them.

And now, Lord, what do I wait for?
My hope is in You.
Deliver me from all my transgressions;
do not make me the reproach of the foolish.
I was mute, I did not open my mouth,
because it was You who did it."[146]

These verses show that David imitated the composure of Jesus Christ revealed to Peter in the second chapter of 1 Peter, in that the injustices done to him did not give birth to bitterness or blame, but rather he held his tongue and humbly engaged in self-reflection. In addition, David entrusted his hope in the Lord, so much so that he realized that God was directly at work in his situation, even through using the wrongs done by others. David was now a seasoned saint who filtered the wickedness of others through the lens of God's grace. The forgiveness David displayed for his adversaries was now rooted in the forgiven-*ness* that

146 Psalm 39:1-9 (NKJV).

he had received from the Lord. It is astonishing to witness the refinement that can take place in one's life when the gift of grace is embraced, in spite of the fact that justice is deserved.

A few years ago, I was given the privilege to pray for a dear man named Andrew who was in one of our local hospitals. Andrew was in his seventies, the patriarch of a wonderful large Italian family in San Diego. He was in a coma as a result of an infection that had spread to a number of his vital organs. When I arrived at his bedside in the Intensive Care Unit, I learned that Andrew's viability had declined critically and that he was soon to be put on life-support. I returned to pray a second time when I received the news that he was not expected to survive. Shortly thereafter, I was given the report from the broken-hearted family that Andrew had succumbed to the infection and had passed away.

But about thirty minutes later, I received a frenzied call from the son where he exclaimed that Andrew had miraculously come back from the dead and that he wanted to speak to me. Indeed, when I returned to the hospital it was verified that this dear man had been medically pronounced dead, but within the hour he awoke and his infection had remarkably disappeared. When I arrived, Andrew called me to his bedside and with a weak whisper he declared to me that he sincerely believed he had died and was given a glimpse of heaven. What he declared shouldn't surprise a believer in the Scriptures, but I must admit at that moment I had goose bumps all over my body. He affirmed that everything the Bible says about heaven is true. And then

Andrew said that he was given a mission from Jesus; though he didn't see Jesus, he believed it was Jesus who spoke to him as he distinctly heard the loving command, "Help children, because the children are suffering."

Though I don't fully understand the significance of his testimony, I do know that his heavenly journey was a profound experience that forever altered his life. My father-in-law also had a similar testimony when he was in his twenties where he died on the operating table after being impaled by rebar following a twenty-five foot fall off of scaffolding. He narrates his experience by explaining how his spirit left his body and how he was able to see the medical staff struggling to revive him.

I have met many skeptics who question God's reality.

I have met many skeptics who question God's reality. For me, I can't deny these very real experiences. Because of God's eternal purposes, He provides Lazarus-type experiences for a select few—and who are we to question His sovereignty?[147] As a chaplain and pastor I have been beside the beds of several individuals who at the moment before their passing have verbally declared in my presence that they were seeing into the heavenlies. I have a number of nurse friends that work in hospice care who confirm similar testimonies of the many they serve who also experience the transition into God's presence. However, what is most frightening to me are the accounts of unbelievers, who, at the point of death, cry out in anguish because of the flames

147 See John 11.

that begin to consume their souls. For some, God provides *near-death* experiences that give the opportunity for people to change the direction of the testimony of their trunk.

Yet for countless others, I have learned that there are multitudes that have *near-life* experiences—God graciously reveals His reality but because of the hardness of hearts and pride, people refuse to receive His redemptive grace. It boggles my mind that people can be so near to eternal life should they simply humble themselves and affirm the Lord's offer to "Confess with your mouth the Lord Jesus and believe in your heart that God has raised Him from the dead, you will be saved. For with the heart one believes and is justified, and with the mouth one confesses and is saved. For the Scripture says, 'Everyone who believes in him will not be put to shame.'"[148]

Are you in that place in your life that you know that God has been making Himself known to you, in perhaps subtle and yet profound ways? Do you want to change the epitaph of your life from what is mortal to a life that is eternal? Take a moment and communicate your heart's profession of faith in God with this simple prayer: "Dear Jesus, I confess to you that I am a sinner and that I have lived outside of your precepts. I repent of my sins and I want to declare from the depth of my heart that you are Lord. I believe in my heart that you died on a cross for me, that you were buried, and after three days you rose from the dead. Please forgive me and come into my heart and empower me with your Holy Spirit to grow in relationship

148 Romans 10:9-11 (ESV).

with You to become the person you want me to be. Enable me now from this day forward to live for Your glory. In Jesus' name, Amen." If you prayed this prayer, God has a trunk-load of love awaiting you for the rest of your life, on into eternity.[149]

Holding on Tight: Things to Consider

GROWING IN GRACE: When recovering from tragedy, studies affirm that the strengthening of one's faith proves to be a key factor for coping and assistance. It follows that prayer and the reading of the Scriptures can bring renewal in difficult seasons. Consider these promises that affirm this truth:

- "Be anxious for nothing, but in everything by prayer and supplication, with thanksgiving, let your requests be made known to God; and the peace of God, which surpasses all understanding, will guard your hearts and minds through Christ Jesus."[150]
- "And let the peace of God rule in your hearts, to which also you were called in one body; and be thankful. Let the word of Christ dwell in you richly in all wisdom, teaching and admonishing one another in psalms and hymns and spiritual songs, singing with grace in your hearts to the Lord."[151]

149 For your next steps in growing your faith, get connected with a Bible teaching church and follow their plan for discipleship. Also, visit www.sdrock.com and select the "Grow" link for growth opportunities. Be sure to download these helpful Apps as well: www.sdrock.com/milesaminute and www.gospelcentral.us

150 Philippians 4:6-7 (NKJV).

151 Colossians 3:15-16 (NKJV).

- "And in His law he meditates day and night. He shall be like a tree planted by the rivers of water, that brings forth its fruit in its season, whose leaf also shall not wither; and whatever he does shall prosper."[152]
- "Therefore we do not lose heart. Even though our outward man is perishing, yet the inward man is being renewed day by day."[153]

PRACTICAL CONSIDERATIONS: A person's foundation of faith generally will correlate to one's wellbeing and happiness. In addition, happier people tend to live a healthier lifestyle. Happy people tend to sleep better, eat better, smoke less, and get more exercise. All of these things contribute to lower heart disease and a longer lifespan. Consider the following suggestions that contribute to happiness and health:

- Grow in one's faith in God.
- Regularly devote focused time with friends and family.
- Express gratitude on a regular basis.
- Practice being more optimistic.
- Engage in frequent acts of kindness.
- Focus on pursuing one's best self.
- Savor joyful events, pleasures and experiences–sanctify the present moment.
- Practice forgiveness as a priority of living.

152 Psalm 1:2-3 (NKJV).

153 2 Corinthians 4:16 (NKJV).

CHAPTER EIGHT

When Right Can Be Wrong

When people travel to San Diego from other parts of the country during the winter months, they are usually treated to our remarkable summer-like weather. Some visitors offer criticism, saying that San Diego misses out on the traditional four seasons. However, I like our summery winters, especially when I am watching the winter weather reports from across the country during horrific winter storms. And if I want to experience winter, I only have to drive an hour up to Julian, a local mountain town, for the day and then I can drive back home to summer for the evening. Nevertheless, we do have a downside to our weather patterns—the lack of rain makes the area vulnerable to wildfires. In fact, we had several very destructive fire seasons, in 2003, 2007, and 2014, when hundreds of homes were lost, and literally millions of residents were evacuated.

During a large-scale disaster, cities and towns experience a number of consistent phases. Cities initially experience a *Rescue Phase,* and then move towards a *Recovery Phase,* and finally transition to a *Closure Phase.* Of course, before any season of disaster, preparedness should be our greatest concern.[154] Should a traumatic event occur, during the *Rescue Phase* there are also a number of sub-phases, such as the *Heroic Phase,* where there is little regard for self-care as people sacrifice for the urgent care of others. There is also the *Honeymoon Phase* as people hold on to hope and pull together as a community, tolerating inconvenience and temporary discomfort. However, eventually things move towards the *Disillusionment Phase* where the harmony fragments and people start to look for someone to blame, and finger pointing becomes pervasive. I have observed these phenomena progress on a consistent basis during many of the disasters wherein I have had the privilege to serve. And as noted previously, the very first disaster of Genesis 3 revealed blameshifting from the get-go.

When we are wronged by the words and actions of others, our bitterness and unforgiveness will continue to do further damage in our lives beyond the initial maltreatment. Learning of God's grace and love for us will free us to sincerely love others despite injustice.

God's grace and love for us will free us to sincerely love others despite injustice.

Relevant to this discussion is the narrative in the ninth chapter of the Gospel of John where Jesus healed a blind man:

154 Readers should be encouraged to visit www.sdrock.com/ministries/disaster/preparedness to download valuable guides for family disaster preparedness.

> "As He passed by, He saw a man blind from birth. And His disciples asked Him, 'Rabbi, who sinned, this man or his parents, that he was born blind?'
>
> Jesus answered, 'It was not that this man sinned, or his parents, but that the works of God might be displayed in him.'"[155]

Here we see the disciples' natural tendency to look for someone to blame for this man's life of hardship. But Jesus surprised the onlookers by asserting that there was no one at fault. Even further, He explained how God graciously used this man's suffering to further reveal the glory of God. It is quite tragic when pious religion blinds people to the beauty of God's grace, especially when the Lord intercedes in uncommon or unexpected ways. Oh, that we could all walk with the simplicity of the miracle of faith as revealed by the blind man's assertion, "One thing I do know, that though I was blind, now I see."[156] The Pharisees were shortsighted in their thinking in that they believed their opinion was right, even at the expense of another's pain.

I received a great education on this theme while serving at the Family Assistance Center (FAC) in the early days following the 9/11 attacks. As crisis chaplains, our team of eight was deployed by the National Transportation Safety Board (NTSB) in collaboration with the American Red Cross to provide care for the family members who were grieving the loss of loved ones impacted by the collapse of the Twin Towers. In the first few days of the 9/11 response,

155 John 9:1-3 (ESV).

156 John 9:25 (ESV).

the FAC was located at the 69th Regiment Armory located at on Lexington Avenue in Manhattan. It was there that we initially served by training and scheduling local clergy to be available to assist the needs of the families who came to the center for information and support. As part of our assignment, we needed to recruit religious leaders from diverse faith backgrounds to provide appropriate care for the variety of personal needs. Initially, we experienced difficulty in securing a team of rabbis to help serve the Jewish families who showed up at the FAC. We had heard that many of the local rabbis were busy serving their own synagogue members. Subsequently, we happened to enlist a retired Rabbi named Bruce who came to the center to volunteer his service. He was a jovial older cleric with a quirky disposition. I immediately clicked with Rabbi Bruce and was given responsibility to oversee his involvement.

There were a few incidents that occurred around my new Jewish friend that almost got the rabbi released from his service at the FAC. A couple of times when we needed Bruce's assistance to help with a few grieving families, we unfortunately were unable to immediately locate him. We discovered that Bruce kept frequenting the special family area where he was found eating at the buffet table and getting shoulder massages. This area was restricted and the crisis workers were not permitted to partake of these services. However, I continued to be an advocate for my eccentric associate, and his involvement was allowed to continue until he eventually crossed the line in a squabble with former president Bill Clinton.

A number of dignitaries made their way into the FAC to provide their support and empathy for the grieving family members. President Clinton and his daughter, Chelsea, were a couple of the early arrivals as they entered a side door next to our chaplaincy post. In fact, our team was the Clintons' first encounter as they began to interact with the FAC workers and guests. The former president and his daughter were very gracious and compassionate, interacting with small groups of family members as they slowly toured the center. Generally, the Clintons would spend a few minutes with each group, briefly hearing their stories and offering condolences. However, at one point I glanced over to see Rabbi Bruce intensely engaged with the president in a lengthy dialogue that seemed to be a bit heated on Bruce's part. Bill Clinton listened intently and gave Bruce his full attention as a crowd gathered around them. Eventually I saw Mr. Clinton stroke Bruce on the back as he exchanged a parting comment and then turned to assist others.

Right relationships are sometimes more important than being right.

When the rabbi made his way back to our area of service, I immediately inquired about the nature of his discussion. Rabbi Bruce repeated to me his passionate tirade with the former president. What he shared with me was pretty much nonsensical and, for sure, quite pointless in the scope of things that would be of interest to President Clinton. I then asked my friend about the response he received from Bill Clinton, to which he stated, "After hearing my suggestions, President Clinton patted me on the back and said, 'Where were you when I needed you in the White House?'" That was genius on the part of the former president—with grace and dignity, Bill Clinton completely affirmed my somewhat quirky friend, without necessarily agreeing with him. Later, I believe the Secret Service wasn't comfortable with Bruce's interchange, as shortly thereafter he was escorted off the premises and his volunteer work on our team was terminated.

Weeks later, President Clinton's wisdom turned out to be a helpful lesson for me in the handling of potential conflict.

When opinions and even worldviews come into dispute, there is a way for love to win.

As a response to the 9/11 aftermath, our church eventually sponsored a special service where we invited a Muslim cleric to have an interfaith exchange with a Christian scholar about the nature of Islamic extremists. The evening seemed to go well. However, after the service a young woman engaged me in a very intense discussion about her discontent with the presentation. Her perspective was that Islam was a violent religion and that we didn't take a strong enough stance to uncover its potential threat. Things heated up, and I concluded that we should just agree to disagree. Shortly thereafter, I made my way to my vehicle where I saw in the distance the young woman overcome with tears as she had engaged someone else about her perspective. "What is wrong with some people?" I thought to myself. After all, I was right in this situation and she was clearly in the wrong. As I got into my car and turned on the ignition, as clear as day, the Lord spoke to my heart as I heard, "Right relationships are sometimes more important than being right." And then my thoughts were instantly directed back to the Family Assistant Center with President Clinton and Rabbi Bruce. Bill Clinton's affirmation of the quirky impassioned rabbi demonstrated how to encourage individuals without necessarily agreeing with them.

I must confess that as a pastor I realized at that moment that I still had a lot to learn, even if it was from what I would consider an unlikely ministry tutor in Bill Clinton. The former president had demonstrated to me a gracious validation of people in the midst of potential conflict and disagreement. When opinions and even worldviews come into dispute, there is a way for love to win.

Since the two greatest commandments are to love God and to love people, love and compassion for others should be dominant in our interactions, no matter how diverse our opinions may be. I am reminded of the statement, "In essentials unity, in non-essentials liberty; in all things charity."[157] Fortunately, the Lord continues to give me ongoing situations where I get the privilege to relearn this precept. Of late, I have observed quite a number of quick-tempered people who have been swift to criticize, assume, judge, or to flat-out blow up over other people's perspectives or efforts. Recently, I actually received an angry criticism from an individual who was distraught that Bible study software was being promoted at a church service as an effort to help people study the Bible more. (Really?)

Paul the Apostle often dealt with conflict, and to the church in Philippi his response was, "Whether in pretense or in truth, Christ is preached; and in this I rejoice, yes, and will rejoice."[158] When individuals came to Jesus having a dif-

---

157 It is often misattributed to St. Augustine of Hippo, but seems to have been first used in 1617 by Archbishop of Split (Spalato) Marco Antonio de Dominis in his work *De Republica Ecclesiastica.*

158 Philippians 1:18 (NKJV).

ferent way of doing things, He stated, "Do not forbid him, for he who is not against us is on our side."[159] Now please hear me. I'm not saying that truth doesn't matter. Paul also wrote, "But even if we, or an angel from heaven, preach any other gospel to you than what we have preached to you, let him be accursed."[160] The virtues of truth and love can at times seem be in tension to each other. Jesus affirmed that the truth of the Gospel would bring division and offense in some of our relationships.[161] But before reacting to others, we need to hear people out, listen, learn, discern, understand, and love. We must always consider the grace shown to us in Christ and then we should seek to reflect that grace back to others. Our response to any potential conflict needs to be seen through the filter of 1 Corinthians 13:

The virtues of truth and love can at times seem be in tension to each other.

> "Love suffers long *and* is kind; love does not envy; love does not parade itself, is not puffed up; does not behave rudely, does not seek its own, is not provoked, thinks no evil; does not rejoice in iniquity, but rejoices in the truth; bears all things, believes all things, hopes all things, endures all things. Love never fails."[162]

I have found that when I take the stance of love, seldom does it fail. I fail, but love never does. Even if you

---

159 Luke 9:50 (NKJV).

160 Galatians 1:8 (NKJV).

161 See Matthew 10:34-39.

162 1 Corinthians 13:4-8 (NKJV).

are right in certain situations, you are wrong if being right attacks another's dignity. Once again, *right relationships* are often more important than *being right.* I am learning to argue less, love more, and enjoy the people I am privileged to serve. Even when personally attacked by others, if I seek to see them through the eyes of Jesus Christ, grace and love will naturally abound. Steven Mosley captured the heart of this virtue when he wrote:

> "Developing a full life is about developing love. Jesus' great summary of the Law expands on love. When it comes to knowing God, we don't get love until we give it to Him. Casual gestures made towards His extravagant grace only immunize us to love's potency. God asks us to respond in kind, not half-heartedly, not absentmindedly, but souled out. So love on your tiptoes, taking in your breath like you've seen the Grand Canyon for the first time. The awe makes you tumble into something so much vaster than yourself."[163]

A research study a few years ago asserted that the mismanagement of injustice can not only lead to you being *dead wrong*, it can also lead you to being *dead.* People with the strongest feelings of being treated unfairly were more than twice as likely to have serious heart disease, heart attacks, or angina in relation to those who seldom deal with injustice at work. Yes, it is unfair when we are treated poorly

163 Mosley, Steven (2002). *Secrets of the Mustard Seed: The Life-Changing Promises From the New Testament.* NavPress, Colorado Springs, CO. Pg. 4.

through inequality and prejudice, and these offensives are just plain wrong. However, when we grow bitter as a result of those inequities, we are further injured through the emotional, mental, and physiological effects of internalized stress. In this way, the person who initially hurt us continues to hurt us through our own internal turmoil. I refer to these experiences as toxic thoughts. The fumes of resentment, cynicism, unforgiveness, revenge, grudges, and animosity escalate as a poison to our mind, body, and soul.[164]

If left unattended, some abuses can continue to reach beyond the grave to assault our hearts.

The book of Hebrews provides counsel in guarding against bitterness: "Pursue peace with all people, and holiness, without which no one will see the Lord: looking carefully lest anyone fall short of the grace of God; lest any root of bitterness springing up cause trouble, and by this many become defiled."[165] In addition, some individuals continue within their bitter torment, even after an antagonist has died. If left unattended, some abuses can continue to reach beyond the grave to assault our hearts as we recall those lethal memories to our own demise.

Shortly after the loss of his son through suicide, Pastor Rick Warren tweeted, "Grieving is hard. Grieving as public figures, harder. Grieving while haters celebrate your pain, hardest. Your notes sustained us." It is incomprehensible that people actually criticized and assaulted Rick and his

164 The Apostle Peter warned a man named Simon who was "poisoned by bitterness." See Acts 8:14-25. For an excellent resource on this subject, consider the book by Dr. Caroline Leaf, *Switch on Your Brain: The Key to Peak Happiness, Thinking, and Health*. Baker Books, Grand Rapids, MI, (2013).

165 Hebrews 12:14-15 (NKJV).

wife, Kay, during their time of deep bereavement and loss. People are horribly cruel at times. However, it is when we are enabled to detach ourselves from the polluted actions and criticisms of others that our hearts are set free to embrace the liberty and renewal that flourishes within God's grace and forgiveness. Through prayer and earnest dependence on the Lord, God will enable you to move beyond the personal disasters caused by others. "Cast your burden on the LORD, and he will sustain you; he will never permit the righteous to be moved."[166] God will send His gracious Holy Spirit to *rescue* our hearts from bitterness, as He leads us to the *recovery* within grace and the *closure* through His love. "The LORD your God in your midst, the Mighty One, will save; He will rejoice over you with gladness, He will quiet you with His love, He will rejoice over you with singing."[167] Being right can be wrong, even to our own hurt.

The ultimate right is to see the Lord in the midst of our interpersonal challenges and to let Him redeem our situations in His love. Let your life be the lyrics of God's song as you put your trust in Him.

Holding on Tight: Things to Consider

GROWING IN GRACE: Forgiveness is a foundational virtue for health and growth in our relationship with God and others. Reflect on these verses and spend time at this present moment to search your heart should there be a root of bitterness where

166 Psalm 55:22 (ESV).

167 Zephaniah 3:17 (NKJV).

forgiveness is needed. Ask for God's strength to lead you into a prayer of forgiveness of others:

- "For if you forgive men their trespasses, your heavenly Father will also forgive you. But if you do not forgive men their trespasses, neither will your Father forgive your trespasses."[168]
- "Get rid of all bitterness, rage and anger, brawling and slander, along with every form of malice. Be kind and compassionate to one another, forgiving each other, just as in Christ God forgave you."[169]
- "Bear with each other and forgive one another if any of you has a grievance against someone. Forgive as the Lord forgave you."[170]
- "Pursue peace with all people, and holiness, without which no one will see the Lord: looking carefully lest anyone fall short of the grace of God; lest any root of bitterness springing up cause trouble, and by this many become defiled."[171]

<u>PRACTICAL CONSIDERATIONS:</u> Toxic thoughts can be many, but so can gracious thoughts. Consider replacing the thoughts of resentment, cynicism, unforgiveness, revenge, grudges, and animosity with the life-giving thoughts of love, good will, sympathy, empathy, respect, favor, affection, kindness, friendliness, delight, calm, and joy.

---

168 Matthew 6:14-15 (NKJV).
169 Ephesians 4:31-32 (NIV).
170 Colossians 3:13 (NIV).
171 Hebrews 12:14-15 (NKJV).

CHAPTER NINE

Mathematics of Joy

Throughout Scripture we are encouraged to cling to God's inner peace and joy, to remember the providence of His ways, even through the most random and harsh experiences that life sends us. Recently, I was called upon to facilitate a follow-up intervention for the emergency crews who responded to a tragic car accident. A sixty-one-year-old man was stopped at a red light when another car suddenly hit him from behind. The driver of the out-of-control car had a seizure, causing his legs to fully extend and push down on the accelerator, resulting in the high-speed crash. It was one of those random incidents where someone was in the wrong place at the wrong time. In an instant, this dear man's life was extinguished. The absurdity of situations like this just doesn't add up within our limited grasp of how the universe would seem to be governed.

The book of Job in the Scriptures directly deals with this quandary without making any excuses for life's difficulties. In his despair, Job came to the conclusion that at times, life seemed to be random. There are situations that occur when apparently good people suffer and evil people prosper. It wasn't until God spoke in Job 38-42 that we hear the Lord's perspective. Once again, God doesn't give us explanations, but rather He clearly asserts His sovereign and majestic ways as being eternally beyond our finite reasoning. Through trials and suffering, God is about cultivating His people to grow within the dimensions of His hope. The Lord instructs us not only to believe in His loving purposes, but also to trust Him through even the most dreadful circumstances. Our pain becomes the means by which God redeems our brokenness, and transforms us into the likeness of His Son.

The equation of God's activities finds its ultimate meaning within His eternal results. Aligning with this concept, the Apostle James boldly wrote:

> "My brethren, count it all joy when you fall into various trials, knowing that the testing of your faith produces patience. But let patience have its perfect work, that you may be perfect and complete, lacking nothing."[172]

Not only are we encouraged to endure hardships, James also declared that we should count it a joy, knowing that God is doing a good work within our character that

---

172 James 1:2-4 (NKJV).

exceeds reason. It is within this perspective of God's sovereignty that we must trust in the Lord's calculations to work all things together for His ultimate good and glory.

The Apostle Paul also confirmed this concept when he declared:

> "Therefore, having been justified by faith, we have peace with God through our Lord Jesus Christ, through whom also we have access by faith into this grace in which we stand, and rejoice in hope of the glory of God. And not only that, but we also glory in tribulations, knowing that tribulation produces perseverance; and perseverance, character; and character, hope. Now hope does not disappoint, because the love of God has been poured out in our hearts by the Holy Spirit who was given to us."[173]

The eternal presence of Jesus Christ becomes our perspective for hope. Hope is the objective reality of being in God's presence forever. And it is this same hope that Jesus anticipated through the suffering He Himself endured.

> "Therefore, since we are surrounded by so great a cloud of witnesses, let us also lay aside every weight, and sin which clings so closely, and let us run with endurance the race that is set before us, looking to Jesus, the founder and perfecter of our faith, who for the joy that was set before him endured the

173 Romans 5:1-5 (NKJV).

cross, despising the shame, and is seated at the right hand of the throne of God."[174]

It is awesome to contemplate that Jesus endured unimaginable suffering, knowing that He would have the joy of being with His heavenly Father for eternity without end. It is also the very means by which Jesus would provide our ultimate joy and our heavenly access through His shed blood. Jesus' example should give us pause to reflect on our priorities in light of our eternal blessings that are often in contrast with our immediate temporal gratification. Years ago a friend of our ministry, Tim Hansel, quipped at a gathering, "Pain is inevitable, but misery is optional. We cannot avoid pain, but we can avoid joy." It becomes our choice to hold fast to the eternal outlook, the conduit for immeasurable joy.

Personal growth experiences in the aftermath of disturbing events far outnumber reports of degenerative disorders.

Many in our day have become familiar with the concept of Post-Traumatic Stress Disorder, where traumatized people may continue to experience stress reactions months after a painful incident. However, there is the flipside to a personal crisis that has been more newly termed Post-Traumatic Growth (PTG). PTG is where people affirm positive benefits directly related to their individual hardship as these experiences can have clarifying and simplifying influences. In fact, studies reveal that personal growth experiences in

174 Hebrews 12:1-2 (ESV).

the aftermath of disturbing events far outnumber reports of degenerative disorders.[175] Some of these Post-Traumatic Growth developments include improved relationships, greater appreciation for life, a sense of personal transformation, as well as new life-lessons learned. However, it should be noted that the good that comes out of the loss doesn't justify or erase the pain that is experienced. Such was the testimony of Dwayne, a seminary student of mine when he was diagnosed with a brain tumor. He was a young father and husband, and I connected with him to pray for his healing and comfort. As he updated me on his progress, I was astounded by his sense of composure and peace. During our conversation he began to narrate his situational outlook as I feverishly took notes, sensing I was in the presence of profound wisdom. He listed seven veracities that he was clinging to during his suffering:

1. Life is a gift from God, savor every moment.
2. My family is made up of the most important people in the world. I need to let them know it and to enjoy them.
3. I need to express all the love and appreciation that God has put into my heart for my friends.
4. Sin is totally repulsive to a holy God.
5. The most important thing in the world is to know Jesus Christ as my Lord and Savior.
6. The greatest purpose and highest fulfillment is in bringing glory to God.

175 See more at: http://www.psychiatrictimes.com/ptsd/posttraumatic-growth-new-perspective-psychotraumatology-0

7. The key to victory in every situation is praise and worship.

As can happen often, I left this encounter being more ministered to by Dwayne, than the ministry I had intended to bring to his hospital room.

In my work in the community responding to human suffering, I have often run into heated individuals who defiantly question God's existence. Once again the age-old question is raised, "If there is a God who is all-loving and all-powerful, why does evil exist?" The question I ask in return is, "If *you* had the power to instantly eliminate evil in the world, would *you* do this?" If so, people need to know that they would have to immediately eliminate their closest friends and family and ultimately remove even their own self as well. Why? Because all people are prone to do wrong from time to time, so for a world to be without evil, every person would need to be eliminated. The beauty of God's promises is that He seeks not to eliminate humanity, but instead He seeks to redeem us.

> "But do not forget this one thing, dear friends: With the Lord a day is like a thousand years, and a thousand years are like a day. The Lord is not slow in keeping His promise, as some understand slowness. Instead He is patient with you, not wanting anyone to perish, but everyone to come to repentance."[176]

176 2 Peter 3:8-9

Yes, God is all-loving and all-powerful, even though evil exists in this world. However, rather than annihilating evil, God is patient to deliver us and to reconcile us through His amazing grace.

The psalmist, Asaph, poured out his heart in honest prayer to the Lord when he admitted his struggles in trying to grasp why God, who is holy, was allowing the wicked to prosper:

> "Surely God is good to Israel,
> to those who are pure in heart,
> but as for me, my feet had almost slipped;
> I had nearly lost my foothold.
> For I envied the arrogant
> when I saw the prosperity of the wicked.
> They have no struggles;
> their bodies are healthy and strong.
> They are free from common human burdens;
> they are not plagued by human ills."[177]

Asaph affirmed that God is good, but His fairness seemed to be in question. In spite of this disheartened viewpoint, the Lord graciously led him to ponder the eternal perspective wherein Asaph was enabled to conclude:

> "When I thought how to understand this,
> it was too painful for me—
> Until I went into the sanctuary of God;

177 Psalm 73:1-5 (NIV).

then I understood their end...
But it is good for me to draw near to God;
I have put my trust in the Lord God,
that I may declare all Your works."[178]

It is within the sanctuary of God's presence that the divine resolve is provided for us to see past our finite limitations of justice and equity.

Personally, I don't believe God gets upset when we occasionally question His sovereign ways. He understands our frailty and limited perspective in a similar way that a dad deals with his own youngster's childish inquiries. I would imagine that the prophet Jeremiah received a gracious nod from the Lord when, in a season of doubt, he asserted:

"Righteous are You O Lord, when I plead with You;
yet let me talk with You about your judgments.
Why does the way of the wicked prosper?
Why are those happy who deal so treacherously?"[179]

Even God's Son, while on the cross, quoted the "Why?" statement of Psalm 22 when He cried out with a loud voice, saying, "My God, My God, why have You forsaken Me?"[180] If Jesus asked *why* within His time of agony, it seems plausible that our heavenly Father has grace for our inquiries when we question our own painful situations.

178 Psalm 73:16-17, 28 (NKJV).
179 Jeremiah 12:1 (NKJV). See also Psalm 10 and Habakkuk for similar themes.
180 Matthew 27:46 (NKJV); cross reference Psalm 22:1.

I have often imagined God's gracious delight extending beyond our human frailties when our childish failures perhaps bring Him a glint of amusement. Such was the situation that arose during a wedding ceremony over which I was presiding. I make it a practice when I meet with an engaged couple to finalize their wedding plans, to assist them in delegating certain responsibilities in relation to the wedding license, rings, and communion elements. For this particular marriage, the groom inadvertently delegated these essential duties to a friend who ended up being somewhat forgetful. Not only had he left the license back at the hotel room, he also forgot to secure the communion bread. As the ceremony was just beginning, the friend ran quickly to the reception area to take care of his oversight. It was a beautiful ceremony, and towards the close of the service, the couple prepared to take communion. As music began to play and we turned toward the altar, I lifted the linen napkin expecting to see a piece of bread. To my surprise, he had secured for the sacrament a slice of chocolate-covered biscotti. I looked over at the befuddled friend, searching for an explanation, and all I received was a shrug of the shoulders. At that moment I sensed that grace warranted a chuckle more than a rebuke. I could only liken this to Ezra's playful exhortation to "eat the fat, drink the sweet,"[181] following the sacred reading of the Law.

---

181 Nehemiah 8:10 (NKJV). It should be noted that Jews were forbidden from eating the rich fats (called *Chelev*), which was to be consecrated to God. The fat was offered as part of the holy sacrifice in the Temple that was wholly for the Lord. See Leviticus 3:16-17, 7:23. The boarder text of Nehemiah 8 demonstrates the grace of a joyful prescription during a holy and sacred moment. "'This day *is* holy to the LORD your God; do not mourn nor weep.' For all the people wept, when they heard the words of the Law. Then he said to them, 'Go your way, eat the fat, drink the sweet, and send portions to those for whom nothing is prepared; for *this* day *is* holy to our Lord. Do not sorrow, for the joy of the LORD is your strength.'" (Nehemiah 8:9b-10 NKJV)

I have observed that there are times when the solemnness of religion can quench joy right out of the soul. One of my mentors in the faith was my friend, author Dr. Sherwood (Woody) Eliot Wirt. Woody always encouraged me that the Christian life was to be a joyful life. Woody was prolific in his writings about the joy of Jesus Christ as a core essential of the Gospel.[182] In his latter years, Woody demonstrated the grace of aging joyfully as he emphasized revering God within one's laughter. Jesus declared, "The thief does not come except to steal, and to kill, and to destroy. I have come that they may have life, and that they may have it more abundantly."[183] The Apostle Paul exhorted, "Godliness is profitable for all things, having promise of the life that now is and of that which is to come."[184] Not only do we have the anticipated joy of eternal bliss with God in heaven, but Paul reaffirmed Jesus' promise that this quality of life was also to be lived in the here and now. Charles Spurgeon once quipped, "When you speak of heaven, let your face light up. When you speak of hell, well then, your everyday face will do."

> There are times when the solemnness of religion can quench joy right out of the soul.

Conversely, many people seem to adopt Charlie Brown's philosophy when times get tough. In a comic strip, Charlie tells Linus his own ideology: "I've developed a new philosophy. I only dread one day at a time."

182 Dr. Wirt's final works were meant to enlighten his readers to the joyful side of Jesus as a Man of joy, playful passion, and a demonstration of life lived to the fullest within His Father's original design. See Sherwood Wirt's books, *Jesus, Man of Joy, The God Who Smiles: An Invitation To A Joy-Filled Life,* and *The Book of Joy: A Treasury of Delights in God.*

183 John 10:10 (NKJV).

184 1 Timothy 4:8 (NKJV).

Even the *Westminster Confession of Faith* encourages us in joy, in that our ultimate purpose is to "glorify God and to enjoy Him forever." The Jews were exceptionally focused on this element of faith. They celebrated numerous annual feasts throughout the year. The feast of Tabernacles, for instance, lasted seven days. They were not to work for seven days, but instead they were told to celebrate.[185] Studies show that happier people are twenty-two percent less likely to develop heart disease. People with the most negative emotions have the highest risk for heart disease, and people who scored highest for happiness had the lowest risk. Happy people tend to sleep better, eat better, smoke less, and get more exercise. All of these things lower a person's risk of heart disease.[186]

Many of us don't learn that Jesus is all we need, until Jesus is all we have.

C.S. Lewis warned the church that there was too much false reverence, "too much speaking in holy tones." When it comes to spiritual things, Billy Graham asserted that people mistakenly think they are to "become sober and quiet, and wear black, and never have a good time, or enjoy a religious event." People cheer at a football game and clap at the circus, but when serving or worshipping the Lord they can at times seem bored. But unquestionably, Jesus Christ is the source of the fullness of joy as declared in the Messianic promise, "You will show me the path of life; in Your presence is fullness of joy; at Your right hand are

185 "You shall keep it as a feast to the LORD for seven days in the year. *It shall be* a statute forever in your generations. You shall celebrate it in the seventh month" (Leviticus 23:41 NKJV). The word "celebrate" in the Hebrew is *khawgag* which means "to move in a circle, to be giddy, to dance."

186 http://www.webmd.com/heart-disease/news/20100217/study-happiness-good-heart

pleasures forevermore."[187] And the joy I am referring to is not mere smiles and happy laughter. Christ's great joy is the inner strength and peace that rejoices even in one's sorrow and pain. Many of us don't learn that Jesus is all we need, until Jesus is all we have.[188] Even our generous giving is to be done with joy. "So let each one give as he purposes in his heart, not grudgingly or of necessity; for God loves a cheerful giver."[189] Robert Louis Stevenson wisely affirmed, "Find out where joy resides, and give it a voice far beyond singing. For to miss the joy is to miss all."

All of this talk of joy may seem absurd to you at this moment, given the anguish of your present situation. In fact, you may be feeling anger as you read through these encouragements that promote joy. This indeed is a very normal reaction as your emotions can be easily triggered when screening your life through the lens of your pain. Though a normal response, this reaction is not usually helpful. Once again, be reminded to think on the things that are true, noble, just, pure, lovely, good, and virtuous,[190] and through God's grace your frustration will be replaced by His peace and, yes, even joy. This is a faithful promise that God has given you in His word.

I tend to believe that the repentant heart is always met with the open arms of a gracious Father, even when

187 Psalm 16:11 (NKJV).

188 For a prescription of joy consider these elements: 1. Joy comes from living in God's presence (Psalm 16:11; Isaiah 40:31; Nehemiah 8:10). If we wait on the Lord, He will renew our strength, and the Joy of the Lord is our strength. 2. Joy comes from the filling of the Holy Spirit and is a fruit of the Spirit (Ephesians 5:17-19, Galatians 5:22, Luke 1:44). 3. Joy comes from knowing and obeying God's Word (John 15:7-11). 4. Joy comes from prayer (John 16:23-24). 5. Joy unspeakable comes from the knowledge of our purpose in life (1 Peter 1:7-9). 6. Supreme Joy is to know that you are loved (Zephaniah 3:17, Hebrews 12:2, John 3:16, Romans 8:38-39). 7. Joy comes from Christian fellowship (Acts 2:46).

189 2 Corinthians 9:7 (NKJV). The Greek word for "cheerful" is *hilaros* from which we derive our word "hilarious."

190 Philippians 4:8-9.

we fail miserably in our immaturity. It is no wonder that God refers to us as His children as He shepherds us as little lambs. This heart perspective was made clear to me through the earnest prayer of a four-year-old during one of our children's Sunday school classes. The youngster looked unusually troubled, and when approached she shared that her beloved grandmother was ill. Tenderly, her teacher offered to pray for her family, but the preschooler insisted that she wanted to lead the prayer. Taking charge, the little child folded her hands and closed her eyes tightly as she cried out a simple prayer of healing for her grandmother. And at the close of her prayer she gave a strong postscript, "In Jesus' name, *two men*!" Naturally the teacher corrected the little one to let her know that the appropriate way to end the prayer was to say "*amen.*" Unconvinced, the four year-old instructed her mentor, "This was an important prayer and I needed more than just one."

One could only laugh at the sincerity of such a child-like outlook. Though she didn't have the right word, this young intercessor had the right heart. In a similar way, we need to know that God sees our hearts when we are living through a season of anguish. Though we surely don't fully grasp the eternal magnitude of our life's experiences within God's providence, we must trust that God is good, even though our situation may question the logic of the moment. It is this foundation of faith that grows our "amen" beyond our circumstances to add up to "more than just one." And it is this sanctuary of hope that will calibrate a depth of joy, even when things just don't seem to add up within our limited reasoning.

Holding on Tight: Things to Consider

GROWING IN GRACE: There's an old adage for relationships that we would be wise to consider: The closer you grow to God, the closer you will grow to one another. This is so simple and yet so very profound. And of course, the fruit of such a pursuit will always display the fruit of the Holy Spirit–"But the fruit of the Spirit is love, joy, peace, longsuffering, kindness, goodness, faithfulness, gentleness, self-control. Against such there is no law."[191] Consider the following encouragements as you draw close to the Lord and let the fruit of His love and joy saturate your life today:

- "Watch, stand fast in the faith, be brave, be strong. Let all that you do be done with love."[192]
- "Therefore be imitators of God as dear children. And walk in love, as Christ also has loved us and given Himself for us, an offering and a sacrifice to God for a sweet-smelling aroma."[193]
- "Then he said to them, 'Go your way, eat the fat, drink the sweet, and send portions to those for whom nothing is prepared; for this day is holy to our Lord. Do not sorrow, for the joy of the LORD is your strength.'"[194]
- "A merry heart makes a cheerful countenance, but by sorrow of the heart the spirit is broken."[195]

---

191 Galatians 5:22-23 (NKJV).

192 1 Corinthians 16:13-14 (NKJV).

193 Ephesians 5:1-2 (NKJV).

194 Nehemiah 8:10 (NKJV)

195 Proverbs 15:13 NKJV

- "A merry heart does good, like medicine, but a broken spirit dries the bones."[196]
- "You will show me the path of life; in Your presence is fullness of joy; at Your right hand are pleasures forevermore."[197]

PRACTICAL CONSIDERATIONS: Sometimes the best thing we can do to dig ourselves out of the pit of despair, is to serve someone else who is also in a great time of need. When you dig someone else out of their problems, you end up with the extra dirt to bury your own hassles. Is there someone in your life who would benefit from your attention? The following suggestions are helpful ideas to assist others who may need your help:

- Encourage their faith and pray for them.
- Be attentive to their needs.
- Listen carefully to them.
- Send a card, text, email or Facebook message to them with a few encouraging Scriptures.
- Invest time with the impacted person.
- Offer your assistance, even if they have not asked for help.
- Validate their perceptions and experiences in a non-judgmental manner.
- Reassure them that they are going to be okay and that they are experiencing normal stress reactions given what they have been through.

196 Proverbs 17:22 (NKJV).
197 Psalm 16:11 (NKJV).

- Protect the individual from the imposition of unhelpful intrusions.
- Help them with everyday tasks like cleaning, cooking, caring for the family, minding children, etc.
- Assist their boundaries and help provide them with some private time.

CHAPTER TEN

Insouciant

It should come as no surprise that in the midst of enduring adversity, there is much potential for anxiety and despair to dominate your life. Discovering your true identity in Jesus Christ empowers you to experience freedom from your fears. I believe the loss of close family members during my childhood contributed greatly to many of my own early insecurities and fears. I distinctly remember lying in bed at night as a child, staring at the ceiling, fearing death, and worrying about the uncertainty of life's future. And whoever came up with the *Now I Lay Me Down to Sleep* prayer—surely the poet had a subtle scheme to torment kids before they fell asleep. Think about it: "Now I lay me down to sleep. I pray the Lord my soul to keep. If I should DIE before I wake, I pray the Lord my soul to take." What a cruel thought to infuse into the little minds of children right before they doze off into their dreams. It wasn't until years later as a growing Christian that I came to the full assurance of my secure heavenly reality through faith in Jesus Christ. It was within my seasoning of faith that my insouciance began to grow.

"Insouciance?" you may ask. Let me explain…

A few years ago I scheduled a lunch appointment with a dear friend, Ken, whose wife was in the last stages of her battle with cancer. On the night before our lunch engagement, I received a call from Ken that his wife had just passed. Respecting his bereavement, I offered to reschedule our lunch for another date. However, he actually preferred to meet as planned, believing it would be helpful. When I arrived at the restaurant the next afternoon, I was blessed to see a couple of other pastor friends that Ken had invited to join us. It is during these raw times of loss that there is a longing to fix a friend's sorrow. But there's no escaping the depth of anguish when the love of your life for over forty years has been taken from you. It's as if the heart has been amputated. There are no quick-fix explanations that will remove the agony of the heart—one doesn't just "get over it." Rather, God enables us to experience His comforts in and through the constantly fluctuating waves of grief. Life adjusts over time to a new normal that can genuinely feel strange at times. The support of friends and family is crucial during these seasons, and it is our supportive presence and practical service that they need far more than any clever platitudes.

There are no quick-fix explanations that will remove the agony of the heart—one doesn't just "get over it."

As the four of us sat around the table, I felt prompted to ask Ken if there were any words that came to mind to describe the many virtues of his wife, Linda. He reflected for a moment and then acknowledged with a sigh that he couldn't even begin to encapsulate all that was in his heart for his beloved wife. Immediately one of the other pastors declared, "Linda was insouciant!" I was puzzled for a moment, not being acquainted with this word. I quickly pulled out my phone to look up the definition of this new addition to my vocabulary. What a great discovery to learn of such a delightful description of my friend. "*Insouciant:* Without anxiety, carefree, lighthearted." We spent the rest of our lunchtime together shifting between tears and laughter as we reminisced over our memories of Linda's insouciant ways. On my drive home that afternoon, I couldn't escape the longing of my heart to become more insouciant. It is now a constant echo in my priorities when faced with life's challenges to choose insouciance over the many other anxious thoughts that compete for a place in my soul. I believe Paul the Apostle understood the foundation of this concept when he wrote:

> "Rejoice in the Lord always. Again I will say, rejoice! Let your gentleness be known to all men. The Lord is at hand. Be anxious for nothing, but in everything by prayer and supplication, with thanksgiving, let your requests be made known to God; and the peace of God, which surpasses all understanding, will guard your hearts and minds through Christ Jesus.

> Finally, brethren, whatever things are true, whatever things are noble, whatever things are just, whatever things are pure, whatever things are lovely, whatever things are of good report, if there is any virtue and if there is anything praiseworthy—meditate on these things."[198]

The choices we make greatly impact our lives. What's more is that our choices are often influenced by our personal outlook and priorities. The novelist, Charles Reade (1814-1884), is accredited with asserting, "Sow a thought, and you reap an act; sow an act, and you reap a habit; sow a habit, and you reap a character; sow a character, and you reap a destiny." Insouciance is a choice of my heart to let go of my own perspectives and to focus on God's providence of grace. Once again we need to *let go and let God.* When we do, our thoughts and actions can be transformed by the influence of God's Holy Spirit towards a destiny of virtue—even within the depths of a crisis.

I have been blessed to know a woman at our church who, despite her hardships, is a living testimony to me of the authentic power of God to transform a life. She was one of seven children who grew up in a rather chaotic home. Her mother had mental illness and was institutionalized when she was just four years old, so my dear friend has very little memory of her mother. Her parents divorced shortly thereafter, and her father quickly

198 Philippians 4:4-8 (ESV).

remarried, followed by another divorce. When she was just eight years old, her mother ended up taking her own life by jumping off the Golden Gate Bridge. As a sixteen-year-old, she dropped out of high school and moved out on her own. As a beautiful young woman, she was allured to the much-publicized pleasures of the Las Vegas nightlife, horse races, and high-end drugs, alongside a number of Hollywood personalities and high rollers. After a number of broken relationships and heartaches, she was often alone with no direction or purpose. Eventually she ended up as a card dealer, engaged to the owner of the card room (who was twenty years her elder), in a crime-ridden area in East San Diego.

On a fateful afternoon, she was looking for something to read while sunning by the pool. Her older brother had recently come to faith in Jesus Christ and had given her a Bible, seeking to influence his sister's faith. Having never read the Bible, it caught her eye that afternoon, and she thought she would check out the New Testament. It was through this simple reading of the Scriptures that a conviction grew within her heart which led her to faith and repentance. Shortly thereafter, she broke off her engagement and began her new life, saturating herself within the Scriptures. A couple of years later I met her at a morning prayer meeting at our church where I quickly recruited her to serve in the children's ministry. I know this woman quite well, because I married her.

This is all part of my wife's amazing story of brokenness giving birth to transformation. I can honestly affirm that Karen is one of the most dynamic revelations to me of

God's life-altering power. If anyone should have a lot of dysfunctional baggage, it should be my wife. However, by the time I met her, the Lord had washed her in His word and had taken her on a remarkable journey of renovation from the inside out. The hardships in her life were many and quite painful, yet these elements didn't define her. I have seen the miracle of God's word, conforming her into the likeness of Jesus Christ. Karen is a profound reflection of 2 Corinthians 5:17-18 where God reveals, "Therefore, if anyone is in Christ, he is a new creation; old things have passed away; behold, all things have become new. Now all things are of God, who has reconciled us to Himself through Jesus Christ, and has given us the ministry of reconciliation" (NKJV).

Every day I am eternally grateful to enjoy the richness of a marriage that reflects the Lord's workmanship and His grace. And God continues to orchestrate His deep work in my wife's growth by giving her a knucklehead husband. We have learned daily that marriage is a gift from God to make us holy and happy, through the refinement of two imperfect people growing more in love with Jesus Christ and with one another. We have experienced the promise of the Christian faith, that the closer we grow to Jesus the closer we grow to each another. I believe that one of God's greatest gifts in life has been to grow older with my best friend, and our marital journey has been enriched with each new season of the lifecycle.[199]

199 Within his final years of despair, King Solomon learned from his misguided pursuits as he exhorted young men to, "Live happily with the woman you love through the fleeting days of life, for the wife God gives you is your best reward down here for all your earthly toil." (Ecclesiastes 9:9 TLB). Solomon's ultimate challenges to respect God and to obey His commandments are worthy precepts to integrate into any relationship of significance.

Though not a doctrinal absolute, I have witnessed that sometimes God saves the best for last, sweetly echoing the Gospel record when Jesus turned water into wine.[200] The expectation of heaven is surely the ultimate fulfillment of this hope. And this affirmation is not due to any absence of hardship, but rather in the way that wine is crafted through crushing, filtering and aging; likewise, relationships can flourish and be transformed through the miraculous work of God's gracious refinement. Perhaps the best advice towards this goal is what I learned from an anniversary card given to me by my wife. On the front of the card it read, "Happy Anniversary, and always remember in a happy marriage there are three ways to do anything: (1) The husband's way. (2) The wife's way. (3) Compromise." When I opened the card I received the wisdom of the ages as it asserted: "Strive for #3, but be prepared to settle for #2."

Many individuals tend to define their identity in relation to their pain.

Contrary to my wife's story, I have observed many individuals who tend to define their identity in relation to their pain. Sadly, at times, people in their brokenness build thick barriers to protect themselves from further hurt. This "protection" is quite understandable, but completely obstructive to potential growth and wellbeing. Since the first sin in the Garden of Eden, people have constructed

200 I have seen the testimony of many God-centered relationships that seem to reflect the narration of the Biblical record in the Gospel of John where Jesus miraculously turned water into wine. "When the master of ceremonies tasted the water that was now wine, not knowing where it had come from (though, of course, the servants did), he called the bridegroom over. 'This is wonderful stuff!' he said. 'You're different from most. Usually a host uses the best wine first, and afterwards, when everyone is full and doesn't care, then he brings out the less expensive brands. But you have kept the best for the last!'" (John 2:9-10 TLB)

layer upon layer of "fig leaves" to create an obstruction from God and others. Our pride drives us to self-protect, and we are naturally inclined to seek to maintain control and power over our lives at all costs. The inner concealed motive is to protect ourselves from additional pain, but the results are sometimes tragic. Various psychoses and relational anomalies are perpetuated as people cling to a dysfunctional identity, as they grow accustomed to the cloak of self-deception. The illusion of control gives birth to false identities which only stiffen the barricades against God's gift of transformation.

It is somewhat of a paradox that Jesus *died* that we might have *life*...

For some, there is a warped defense mechanism that accommodates enduring pain because they feel they deserve the suffering in relation to their guilt or shame—sort of a divinely sought-after payback in relation to their sinful failures. For others, complex behaviors and character traits are derived that give rise to a pseudo-self which seeks to project an external image that is inconsistent with their internal reality. As a result, people live a lifetime of lies and deception primarily fooling themselves more than those they are seeking to deceive.

Trying to act like we "have it all together" despite our complex dysfunctions tends to thwart the work of grace. Complicating things further, some individuals develop a victim mentality where they see themselves as powerless. This is a learned behavior from repeated experiences throughout one's upbringing when core physical, psychological, and sociological needs for safety, love, and personal worth are not adequately met. As a result, people can develop a dysfunctional, entitled perspective, believing that others are responsible to fulfill their needs as they manipulate through blameshifting, complaining, and rationalizing to gain control of their situations.[201] Indulged self-pity only deepens the wounds and extends the suffering.

Jesus declared that to find our life, we must be willing to lose our life; he who loses his life for Christ's sake shall find life.[202] He asserted, "I have come that they may have life, and that they may have *it* more abundantly. I am the good shepherd. The good shepherd gives His life for the sheep."[203] It is somewhat of a paradox that Jesus *died* that we might have *life*, and by grace through faith we are empowered to *die* that we might have His *life*. In his teaching about the nature of the law Paul the Apostle declared:

> "For I through the law died to the law that I might live to God. I have been crucified with Christ; it is no longer I who live, but Christ lives in me; and the life which I now live in the flesh I live by faith in the Son of God, who loved me and gave Himself for me. I do not set aside the grace of God; for if righteousness comes through the law, then Christ died in vain."[204]

201 In relation to this concept there is an amazing testimony of Jesus healing a man at the Pool of Bethesda who had an infirmity for thirty-eight years and was unable to walk. When Jesus asked the man if he wanted to be made well, the sick man answered with an excuse as to why he couldn't be made well. Yet in spite of this man's excuses, Jesus compassionately healed him. See John 5:1-15.

202 "And he who does not take his cross and follow after Me is not worthy of Me. He who finds his life will lose it, and he who loses his life for My sake will find it" (Matthew 10:18-39 NKJV).

203 John 10:10-11 (NKJV).

204 Galatians 2:19-21 (NKJV).

What freedom we discover when we allow the Lord to peel away the corpse of our false identities and to bring forth our true identity in Jesus Christ. Throughout the New Testament, God's children are declared to be saints as the Lord frees us from our past. Through the victory of the cross, God's righteousness is attributed to us, and His nature becomes our true nature. We are declared to be complete in His Son and we are destined for our glorification in heaven.[205] To live within the authority of this reality sets us free from the many illusions of control and false identities that plague our souls. The Lord provides assurance when He reveals that "if God is for us, who can be against us? …in all these things we are more than conquerors through Him who loved us."[206] We need to be reminded always that the Lord already sees us seated with Him in heavenly places.[207]

It was such a delight to receive an elated email from a church friend about her newly-embraced freedom in Jesus Christ. Her story was one of great pain that included the betrayal of an adulterous husband. However, by the mercy and empowerment of God this couple was able to work through their wounds and failures to build a restored marriage. It was a few years later that this dear woman made a commitment to be baptized at one of our church baptisms in San Diego's Mission Bay. The baptism was to take place

205 "For in Him dwells all the fullness of the Godhead bodily; and you are complete in Him, who is the head of all principality and power" (Colossians 2:9-10 NKJV). "But God, who is rich in mercy, because of His great love with which He loved us, even when we were dead in trespasses, made us alive together with Christ (by grace you have been saved), and raised us up together, and made us sit together in the heavenly places in Christ Jesus, that in the ages to come He might show the exceeding riches of His grace in His kindness toward us in Christ Jesus" (Ephesians 2:4-7 NKJV).

206 Romans 8:31, 37 (NKJV).

207 Ephesians 2:6

on June 10th that year, and she had gained prior permission to have her husband join the pastors in baptizing her. Yet, on the morning of June 10th she began the day in a funk, growing increasingly anxious and irritable. At one point she was going to delay this commitment until a later date. For some reason she was feeling uneasy and unsettled, and she was becoming increasingly annoyed. Deep within her heart were wounds that were bleeding but she wasn't discerning their source. As the afternoon progressed she eventually took time out to sit and pray through her feelings. In this moment of silence, God whispered to her heart as she revisited her past hurt and came to realize that years earlier it was on June 10th that her husband's infidelity was disclosed to her. The thick scabs on her soul were so veiled that she had developed an avoidant trigger that was setting off a mixed alarm in her life to fight, take flight, or freeze. Her psychological defense mechanisms went beyond her cognizance, which is actually surprisingly common for people recovering from past grievances. Her feelings were very real, but not necessarily based on a present reality. Once realized, she took the authority given to her in Christ to choose life and freedom from her past wounds. She chose to give June 10th new meaning as she was enabled to redefine her past. Overcome by God's love, June 10th now signifies to her the new meaning of her identification with Jesus Christ in baptism. My friend realized that not only had her sin been conquered by the death, burial, and resurrection of Jesus Christ, but also her past hurts could be buried with Jesus Christ in baptism. She had been resurrected in her baptism to the freedom from the dark grave of her husband's adultery. This date now is a trigger of new life as the old is gone and all has become new.

So true is Jesus' declaration over our sin when He said, "Therefore if the Son makes you free, you shall be free indeed."[208] We must cease trying to portray a false reality, of appearing that we have it all together and are in control. When we die to this lie, we realize that true life and meaning comes from an abiding and vibrant relationship with the living God. It is in Christ that we discover our significance, and it is in Him that our identity is founded. This truth is actually a major theme within the New Testament. Life in and through Jesus Christ is mentioned over thirty times in Paul's letter to the Ephesians, and over 216 times throughout the New Testament.

It is in Christ that the soul is released from all of the anxieties that afflict us on this side of heaven. It is in Christ that insouciance can grow within you, even through those moments of your life when uncertainty and agitating thoughts crowd into your mind and heart. May the Lord give you a testimony of insouciance as you embrace His grace as the filter of your past, your present, and your future.

Holding on Tight: Things to Consider

GROWING IN GRACE: The Scriptures encourage us to "Be still and know that I am God."[209] It is within this truth that we can genuinely be without anxiety, carefree, and lighthearted. Knowing

---

208 John 8:36 (NKJV).

209 Psalm 46:10 (NIV).

that God is in control over all your circumstances should quiet your soul and bring rest to all of your anxious thoughts. As a result, you should rest easier and even sleep more soundly. In fact, the quality of sleep is strongly correlated with good health and proper stress management. Take fifteen minutes out of your busy schedule today and pray that the Lord would make you more insouciant. Also pray that Jesus would increase the rest for your soul and the much-needed sleep for your body. The Bible encourages our restful state of being:

- "Yes, my soul, find rest in God; my hope comes from him."[210]
- "Return to your rest, my soul, for the LORD has been good to you."[211]
- "It is vain for you to rise up early, to sit up late, to eat the bread of sorrows; for so He gives His beloved sleep."[212]
- "The sleep of a laboring man is sweet, whether he eats little or much."[213]

PRACTICAL CONSIDERATIONS: In addition to the strengthening of your faith, there are some very sensible things you can do to improve your sleep patterns. If you are not sleeping well, consider these suggestions:

- Maintain regular sleep routines as much as possible. Go to bed at a consistent time.

210 Psalm 62:5 (NIV).
211 Psalm 116:7 (NIV).
212 Psalm 127:2 (NKJV).
213 Ecclesiastes 5:12 (NKJV).

- Don't eat or drink much before bedtime.
- Avoid caffeine and nicotine.
- Take shorter daytime naps.
- Exercise during the day, but not right before bed.
- Cool your bedroom down. People sleep better in a cooler room with more blankets than in a warm room with just a sheet.
- Consider taking a warm bath or shower before bed. An occasional soaking in a hot tub or Jacuzzi will help.
- Control distracting noises.
- Subtle ambient noise can eliminate annoying sounds and lull a person to sleep (e.g. white noise, the hum of a fan or air conditioning unit).

CHAPTER ELEVEN

Then You Shall Know

One of the greatest gifts of wisdom that a pastor gave to me early in my marriage was to read through the Bible out loud together with my bride. Karen and I took up this challenge—not as a duty or obligation, but as a time of enrichment and intimate fellowship—and it has been one of the most cherished joys of our relationship. We start each day in the Scriptures and prayer as we sip our coffee and share about the things of God. In our thirty-five years of marriage, we continue daily to experience God's leading for each day's enrichment for our souls. It was during one of these morning devotional times that the Lord revealed to us for the first time a phrase that is repeated throughout the Scriptures. It is a profound thread of truth that reveals God's heart for His people to truly know Him even within hardship. It's a phrase that God declares hundreds of times in both the

Old and New Testaments. The statement is this: "Then you shall know that I am the Lord." Over and over again throughout Scripture, God affirms that He is present in all of life's circumstances, and it is often in hardship that He is most vocal in making His presence known.

This declaration is first discovered when God strengthened Moses to lead His people out of Egypt:

> "God spoke to Moses and said to him, 'I am the LORD. I appeared to Abraham, to Isaac, and to Jacob, as God Almighty, but by My name the LORD I did not make myself known to them. I also established My covenant with them to give them the land of Canaan, the land in which they lived as sojourners. Moreover, I have heard the groaning of the people of Israel whom the Egyptians hold as slaves, and I have remembered My covenant. Say therefore to the people of Israel, "I am the LORD, and I will bring you out from under the burdens of the Egyptians, and I will deliver you from slavery to them, and I will redeem you with an outstretched arm and with great acts of judgment. I will take you to be My people, and I will be your God, and you shall know that I am the LORD your God, who has brought you out from under the burdens of the Egyptians."'"[214]

Throughout the Bible we learn that in times of blessings and in times of challenge, God is always present, making

214 Exodus 6:2-7 (ESV).

Himself known. God's covenant of grace is one of relationship where we become His people and He becomes our God. And within this covenantal relationship the Lord wants us to know His ever-present help in times of need.[215] It is within His presence that we can experience the fullness of life as God makes Himself known in every situation. It was during the plagues in Egypt and other national events that God's people would know that YHWH is God.[216] The Lord also promised to make Himself known through His fulfilled promises and blessings.[217]

Immanuel means "God *with* us!" What an amazing concept!

Many are perhaps familiar with the Messianic Scripture: "Therefore the Lord Himself will give you a sign: behold, the virgin shall conceive and bear a Son, and shall call His name Immanuel."[218] Immanuel means "God *with* us!" What an amazing concept! The God of the universe desires to have a relationship *with* us through His beloved Son. Isaiah 7:14 possibly conjures up thoughts of Christmas or maybe a childhood memory of an old Sunday school felt-board story. However, these wonderful memories can be in danger of drifting into an idle place of empty tradition and religious familiarity. People can end up missing one of the most dynamic and intimate revelations from the very heart of God.

---

215 "God *is* our refuge and strength, a very present help in trouble" (Psalm 46:1 NKJV).

216 YHWH is a form of the Hebrew name of God used in the Bible. YHWH was traditionally a name too sacred to be uttered, and therefore, without vowels the sound of God's name is uncertain. See Exodus 6:7; 14:4, 18; Ezekiel 5:13, 6:7-14. In Ezekiel this declaration is repeated throughout the book over seventy times, primarily in relation to judgment.

217 Exodus 10:3; 16:6, 12; 29:46; 31:13; Deuteronomy 29:6; Joshua 3:10; 4:24; Ezekiel 16:62.

218 Isaiah 7:14 (NKJV).

I believe that one of the greatest challenges to an authentic relationship with God is the slumber of empty religion. By that, I mean to define religion as a set of customs and rituals that are externally experienced by many who only have a casual, mental acknowledgment of God's existence. Individuals can slip into a dreary routine of occasional church attendance, lacking a genuine, deep, abiding relationship *with* Jesus Christ. How grateful we should be to know and enjoy God and the intimate communion He longs to have with us. He simply wants to be *with* us and to transform us into the likeness of His Son. On the other hand, there is that dangerous place where people take part in a religion that tries to work its way into God's acceptance, living under a sense of obligation, guilt, and shame.

One of the greatest challenges to an authentic relationship with God is the slumber of empty religion.

From Genesis to Revelation, the Bible consistently reveals to the people of faith that the Lord desires to be *with* us. In the Garden of Eden, God sought to be *with* Adam and Eve as He walked in the cool of the day.[219] In Revelation, God's tabernacle is "*with* men and He will dwell *with* them and they shall be His people, God Himself will be *with* them and be their God."[220] In fact, one could easily surmise that the entire Bible can be summed up as a narrative of the eternal omnipotent God creating the entire universe for His glory, and at the heart of His purposes is His desire to be in intimate relationship *with* His people.

219 Genesis 3:8.

220 Revelation 21:3 (NKJV) emphasis mine.

It was in another garden—Gethsemane—that Jesus prayed for our union and oneness that parallels the oneness of marriage, "that they may be one just as We are one: I in them, and You in Me; that they may be made perfect in one, and that the world may know that You have sent Me, and have loved them as you have loved Me."[221] As Jesus proclaimed the Great Commission to His disciples He promised, "I am *with* you always, even to the end of the age."[222] And not only does Jesus long to be *with* us, the Scriptures reveal that God is *for* us, *in* us, and that He seeks to come *upon* us in His fullness.[223] Knowledge of this divine intention of relationship sets us free from the burden of compulsory religion. No matter what life throws at us, God longs for us to know that He is with us to deliver us; it is then that we shall know that *YHWH* is God.[224]

No matter what life throws at us, God longs for us to know that He is with us to deliver us.

Perhaps related to the core of this truth is God's self-disclosure of His name when He spoke to Moses out of the burning bush. God initiated His intentions and asserted:

> "I will certainly be *with* you… Then Moses said to God, 'Indeed, when I come to the children of Israel and say to them, "The God of your fathers has sent me to you," and they say to me, "What is His name?"

221 John 17:22-23 (NKJV).

222 Matthew 28:20 (NKJV) emphasis mine. For other "with" themes see: Genesis 28:15, 31:3, 46:4; Exodus 3:12; Deuteronomy 31:8, 23; Joshua 1:5, 9; Judges 6:12; 1 Samuel 10:7; 1 Kings 8:57; 1 Chronicles 28:20; 2 Chronicles 1:1, 20:17; Psalm 23:4, 118:6; Isaiah 41:10, 43:2, 5; Jeremiah 1:8, 19, 15:20, 20:11, 42:11, 46:28; Ezekiel 43:9; Haggai 1:13, 2:4; Zechariah 8:23, 10:5; Matthew 1:23, 18:20; Hebrews 13:5.

223 Psalm 56:9; Romans 8:31; Ephesians 3:17; Colossians 1:27; Isaiah 59:21; Acts 1:8, 10:44, 11:15, 19:6.

224 See Joshua 1:9, 3:7; Jeremiah 1:8, 19, 16:21.

> what shall I say to them?' And God said to Moses, "I AM WHO I AM.' And He said, 'Thus you shall say to the children of Israel, "I AM has sent me to you."'"[225]

The ever-present I AM promised to be *with* Moses in every situation that he would face through the victories and challenges that lay ahead. Throughout the Old Testament God revealed that He is *with* us as our Healer (*YHWH Rapha*), Peace (*YHWH Shalom*), Provider (*YHWH Yireh)*, Banner (*YHWH Nissi*), Righteousness (*YHWH Tsidkenu*), Presence (*YHWH Shammah)* and our Shepherd (*YHWH Raah)*.[226] In every situation, God's name reveals His living presence in the fulfillment of His promises. Similarly in the Gospel of John, Jesus revealed His own "I am" declarations to continue the promises of God to the church. Jesus declared: "I AM the bread of life; the light of the world; the door; the good shepherd; the resurrection and the life; the way, the truth, and the life; and the true vine."[227] What a joy it is to discover God's presence in every situation we experience, every day.

In His name—YHWH, or I AM—and the descriptions of his character (healer, provider, the light of the world), His eternal qualities come alive that we would know that the Lord alone is God, and that He is near to uphold us throughout the circumstances of life.

In addition, God's people benefit when they embrace the power and authority He bestows upon us in the name

---

225 Exodus 3:12-14 (NKJV. Emphasis mine).

226 Exodus 15:26; Judges 6:24; Genesis 22:14; Exodus 17:15; Jeremiah 23:6; Ezekiel 48:35; Psalm 23:1.

227 John 6:48; 8:12; 10:9, 11; 11:25; 14:6; 15:1 (NKJV).

of Jesus. Jesus promised us, "Most assuredly, I say to you whatever you ask the Father in My name He will give you. Until now you have asked nothing in My name. Ask and you will receive, that your joy may be full."[228] The power of God's name was also revealed when Jesus asserted, "I am," at His arrest in Gethsemane as the soldiers drew back and fell to the ground.[229] This authority should be no surprise to us as the Scriptures reveal, "Therefore God also has highly exalted Him and given Him the name which is above every name, that at the name of Jesus every knee should bow, of those in heaven, and of those on earth, and of those under the earth, and that every tongue should confess that Jesus Christ is Lord, to the glory of God the Father."[230] The grandeur of God's name and His ways should give us a sense of pervasive hope, because no matter how overwhelming our situation is for the moment, God IS and He will be *with* us to accomplish His good and gracious pleasure.

I am reminded of an old lyric composed by the hymn writer, Fredrick Faber (1814-1863) that has enriched my life over the years, "Only to sit and think of God, Oh, what a joy it is! To think the thought, to breathe the Name, Earth has no higher bliss."[231] We should be encouraged to continually have the Lord's name on our lips, as He is closer to us than our very thoughts.

At this point, I am also reminded of how special my own name is. It was on a Sunday morning that I received

---

228 John 16:23-24 (NKJV).

229 John 18:6.

230 Philippians 2:9-11 (NKJV).

231 http://www.cyberhymnal.org/htm/m/y/mygodhow.htm

a blessing to learn that my name, Mickey, was revered by the young of God's flock. One of our church leaders shared with me that his family had a weekly Saturday night bedtime routine to pray for the church and the pastors. On this one particular evening, their five-year old concluded his prayer time with a specific blessing for his pastors. The little guy prayed, "God bless Pastor Miles, God bless Pastor Mike, and God bless Pastor Mickey and Pluto and Goofy!" It was an honor to hear of such a lofty blessing bestowed upon me amongst such a prestigious group of saints.

It is through a daily diet of the Scriptures that our hearts are enlightened to know the Lord more intimately. Our ultimate pursuit in life should be to really know and experience the Lord. Paul the Apostle boldly proclaimed:

> "Indeed, I count everything as loss because of the surpassing worth of knowing Christ Jesus my Lord. For His sake I have suffered the loss of all things and count them as rubbish, in order that I may gain Christ and be found in Him, not having a righteousness of my own that comes from the law, but that which comes through faith in Christ, the righteousness from God that depends on faith—that I may know Him and the power of His resurrection, and may share His sufferings, becoming like Him in his death, that by any means possible I may attain the resurrection from the dead."[232]

232 Philippians 3:8-10 (ESV).

Similarly, Moses had a longing to experience God more intimately when he declared,

> "See, You say to me, 'Bring up this people; but You have not let me know whom You will send with me. Yet You have said, 'I know you by name, and you have also found favor in My sight.' Now therefore, if I have found favor in your sight, please show me now Your ways, that I may know You in order to find favor in Your sight. Consider too that this nation is Your people. And He said, 'My presence will go with you, and I will give you rest."[233]

King David wrote, "One thing I have desired of the Lord, that will I seek: that I may dwell in the house of the Lord all the days of my life, to behold the beauty of the Lord, and to inquire in His temple."[234] Make it your primary focus of each day to *know*, to *grow* and to *go* for the Lord as you seek and serve Him throughout each day's pursuits.

One Easter Sunday afternoon, my family journeyed a couple hours north to visit my father and stepmother for a family dinner. During our visit, I was given the assignment to sift through an old dresser in my parents' garage to see if there was anything I wanted before it was given to the Salvation Army. The drawers were overflowing with old family pictures and mementos that ended up filling drawers in my garage. Of significance, however, was the finding of an old termite-eaten black book, which at first

233 Exodus 33:12-14 (ESV).

234 Psalm 27:4 (NKJV).

glance, I thought to be a Bible. As I opened to the first page, to my delight I discovered that this book was actually my mother's five-year diary dating back to 1934. It was a record of her daily thoughts and experiences as an adolescent. None of my family had been aware of this book's existence, and it has become a treasure to us all. Within the pages of this narrative I discovered my mom's faith in God and her love for her father.[235]

I also read exploits of life in Southern California as a teenager. Since my mother passed away while I was still pretty young, this diary became a cherished gift that acquainted me with a very special woman, to know her thoughts, desires, history and beliefs. That night as I lay in bed reading through my mom's diary entries, I couldn't help but see a parallel to my black leather Bible on my nightstand. In a sense, I discovered at that moment that the Bible was my heavenly "Parent's" diary made available to all of His children. Within the pages of God's narrative, we learn of His thoughts, desires, history, and truths. Within His revelation we receive the cherished gift to intimately acquaint ourselves with our Lord.

Within the pages of God's narrative, we learn of His thoughts, desires, history, and truths.

God knows each of us intimately. The Lord affirms that He knew us before the foundation of the world and that He knows every detail of our life.[236] Yet, God also

235 Throughout the diary, my mom actually used the endearing term, "daddy." She narrated many dates to the theater with her daddy as she recorded numerous tales of her familial affection, but especially highlighted her daddy-daughter bond.

236 Ephesians 1:4; Psalm 139.

desires to be known and to disclose the depth of His love for us. The Lord declared to Jeremiah: "You will seek Me and find Me, when you seek Me with all your heart."[237] When a person seeks to truly know God, the Lord promises to make Himself known.

Personally, I believe that God is constantly speaking and revealing Himself throughout every moment of every day; we just need to listen. Paul the Apostle declared to the people of Athens, "From one man He made all the nations, that they should inhabit the whole earth; and He marked out their appointed times in history and the boundaries of their lands. God did this so that they would seek Him and perhaps reach out for Him and find Him, though He is not far from any one of us. 'For in Him we live and move and have our being.'"[238]

If I'm attentive in the morning when I wake up and turn on the lights, I hear the Lord declare, "I am the light of the world."[239] When my feet touch the floor, I am reminded, "Nevertheless the solid foundation of God stands, having this seal: 'The Lord knows those who are His.'"[240] I often hear the morning birds outside of my window and the Lord whispers, "Look at the birds of the air, for they neither sow nor reap nor gather into barns; yet your heavenly Father feeds them. Are you not of more value than they?"[241] I get a glass of water and God speaks, "If anyone thirsts, let

237 Jeremiah 29:13 (ESV).
238 Acts 17:26-28 (NIV).
239 John 8:12 (NKJV).
240 2 Timothy 2:19 (NKJV).
241 Matthew 6:26 (NKJV).

him come to Me and drink."[242] When on my way to work I see the broad and narrow roads that constantly remind me of the two eternal destinies.[243] The trees speak of God's Kingdom, the grass promises His provision, the breeze on my face instructs me on the ways of the Holy Spirit, and the sun, moon, and stars shout to me of God's glorious handiwork.[244] God makes Himself known in our marriage and family, as these are simply wondrous gifts to discover and discern His centrality to all human relationships. If we are attentive, we can perceive God's presence in all that we do and in everything we experience. And of course, above all of God's disclosures of His nature is the ultimate revelation through His Son Jesus Christ:

> "Long ago, at many times and in many ways, God spoke to our fathers by the prophets, but in these last days He has spoken to us by His Son, whom He appointed the Heir of all things, through Whom also He created the world. He is the radiance of the glory of God and the exact imprint of His nature, and He upholds the universe by the word of His power. After making purification for sins, He sat down at the right hand of the Majesty on high."[245]

God is passionate about revealing His perfections, as there is no greater joy in our human existence than to

242 John 7:37 (NKJV).

243 Matthew 7:13-14.

244 Matthew 13:31-32; Matthew 6:30; John 3:8; Psalm 8, 19.

245 Hebrews 1:1-3 (ESV).

know, and be known by, our gracious Savior.[246] His love is unfathomable, His glory is limitless, and His lofty wonder is indescribable as the Sovereign King of Kings and Lord of Lords. And beyond human understanding, God desires a personal relationship with His beloved children. As such, it is magnificently mysterious that at every moment of every day God delights in fully disclosing glimpses of His ever-present reality. No greater pleasure and no greater experience are bestowed upon men and women than to embrace the heart of God and His intended purposes. Though written centuries ago, Henry Scougal's words ring true through the ages when he declared,

> "The worth and excellency of a soul is to be measured by the object of its love. We are most satisfied when we seek God's pleasure above our own, and we gradually become conformed to what we most love and admire. We do not exist for ourselves—we exist for the Father and through the Son. Our souls become emaciated when our pleasure is affixed to position, possessions, and power, because these things are destined to corrupt and perish."[247]

In God alone is our heart satisfied, and it is within His divine love that we know what authentic love is. To know

---

246 Within this theme of relational knowing, Jesus asserted, "I am the good Shepherd; and I know My sheep, and am known by My own. As the Father knows Me, even so I know the Father; and I lay down My life for the sheep." (John 10:14-15 NKJV). God revealed to Paul the Apostle that there will be a time in the future where this relational knowledge will be realized in its ultimate sense. "When I was a child, I spoke as a child, I understood as a child, I thought as a child; but when I became a man, I put away childish things. For now we see in a mirror, dimly, but then face to face. Now I know in part, but then I shall know just as I also am known. And now abide faith, hope, love, these three; but the greatest of these *is* love." (1 Corinthians 13:11-13 NKJV).

247 Scougal, Henry. (2012; originally, 1677) *The Life of God in the Soul of Man*. Rough Draft Printing, Seaside, OR. p.11.

this, is to quiet the soul and to cease all strivings for pursuits that will never satisfy. One can only assume that it was the majestic and lofty wonder of God that lifted the Apostle Paul into the heavenlies when he penned:

> "For this reason I bow my knees to the Father of our Lord Jesus Christ, from whom the whole family in heaven and earth is named, that He would grant you, according to the riches of His glory, to be strengthened with might through His Spirit in the inner man, that Christ may dwell in your hearts through faith; that you, being rooted and grounded in love, may be able to comprehend with all the saints what is the width and length and depth and height—to know the love of Christ which passes knowledge; that you may be filled with all the fullness of God. Now to Him who is able to do exceedingly abundantly above all that we ask or think, according to the power that works in us, to Him be glory in the church by Christ Jesus to all generations, forever and ever. Amen."[248]

God is beyond knowledge but is knowable, He is forever holy but is approachable, He is infinitely righteous but is compassionate, and He is eternally God but came to us as a Man. As you seek His presence amidst our greatest triumphs and through your most desperate heartbreaks, Jesus will saturate your existence with His Spirit and *then you*

248 Ephesians 3:14-21 (NKJV).

will know that He is God. Even now at this very instant, no matter what your desperation might be, God is with you. He wants you to know His reality, presence, and comfort in the midst of your anguish, and He will whisper, or even shout to you, what you need to know for the moment. Take to heart the following encouragements as you open your life to God's personal wisdom for you.

Holding on Tight: Things to Consider

GROWING IN GRACE: The Psalmist wrote, "Let them give thanks to the LORD for his unfailing love and His wonderful deeds for men, for He satisfies the thirsty and fills the hungry with good things."[249] It is good to give thanks to the Lord for all his goodness towards you. Pause right now and from the depth of your heart, give thanks to God for His grace and the many things with which He has blessed you. " Rejoice always, pray without ceasing, in everything give thanks; for this is the will of God in Christ Jesus for you."[250] "Oh, give thanks to the LORD, for He is good! For His mercy endures forever."[251]

PRACTICAL CONSIDERATIONS: Here are a number of suggestions to develop an attitude of gratitude. Identify two items from this list that you will engage in today:

- Intentionally say, "thank you" as frequently as possible.

249 Psalm 107:8-9 (NIV).

250 1 Thessalonians 5:16-18 (NKJV).

251 Psalm 107:1 (NKJV). Also repeated again in Psalm 107:8, 15, 21 and 31.

- Acknowledge the small blessings in your life. Consider the simple things that are often overlooked.
- Look on the positive side of a current issue rather than focusing on the negative.
- Start a journal of thanksgiving. At the end of every day write down the things that occurred for which you are thankful.
- Share with others what you are thankful for about them. Verbalizing our gratitude encourages a positive outlook.

CHAPTER TWELVE

When God is Silent

Sometimes life makes no sense. We find ourselves in situations we cannot understand within the finite realm of logic. These times can be dark, ominous, frightening, isolating, with no rational explanations for our burdened souls. During these seasons—when it seems like God is silent to our circumstances—is when His Word invites us to trust, hope, and believe in the goodness of God.

This is the mystery of faith.

Let's go on a little stroll together through the encouragements in Scripture about the times when life doesn't seem to make sense. Before we do though, I need to review another fascinating word that theologians and philosophers have devised that may provide a fresh perspective. It's the word *antinomy.* It is a word which much smarter people than me have conjured up to label the things that they can't explain. Immanuel Kant (1724-1804) used this term to describe equally true entities that apparently contradict each other. It is when empirical reason—what we can observe, test, and prove—is exceeded by the transcendence of two or more truths that are in opposition to each other. For example, the Trinity of God is an antinomy. The humanity and divinity of Jesus Christ is an antinomy. For me, the goodness and graciousness of God within human suffering is an antinomy. Within classical theology, we can explain the origin of sin, human failure, and the resulting pain (i.e. theodicy), but even with these explanations, my mind and my heart still seem to be in opposition to one another. Even more so, when in the midst of the horrific pain of a toddler dying from brain cancer, or the emotional torture of adultery, the logic of it all breathes of antinomy.

> Why are some people so amazingly blessed while others go through such repulsive circumstances?

So peculiar was the afternoon when I received two phone calls from church members that were seconds apart. The first call informed me of a husband's death, while moments later the phone rang again, and a young father excitedly announced the birth of his firstborn son. One departs, one arrives. Similar was the occasion when a woman gave birth to her first child at the same hospital where her father lay in the temporary morgue having passed away from a heart attack just hours before. One departs, one arrives. Life can be weird at those moments! Though these may not be true antinomies, they are strange nonetheless.

David was well-acquainted with these concepts; at least fifty-two of the Psalms deal with grief and suffering, and many more bleed with the questions of an ailing heart in the presence of a loving God. David cried:

> Why do You stand afar off, O Lord?
> Why do You hide in times of trouble…
>
> How long, O Lord? Will You forget me, forever?
> How long will You hide Your face from me?
> How long shall I take counsel in my soul,
> having sorrow in my heart daily?
> How long will my enemy be exalted over me?[252]

The entire book of Job also abounds with this query:

> Why did I not die at birth?
> Why did I not perish when I came from the womb?
>
> My soul loathes my life;
> I will give free course to my complaint,
> I will speak in the bitterness of my soul.
> I will say to God, 'Do not condemn me;
> show me why You contend with me.'
>
> Why do You hide Your face,
> and regard me as Your enemy?[253]

Why?!!!

---

252 Psalm 10:1, 13:1-2 (NKJV).
253 Job 3:11, 10:1-2, 13:24 (NKJV).

On the complete other end of the spectrum, why are some people so amazingly blessed while others go through such repulsive circumstances? The Scriptures decree, "The blessing of the Lord makes one rich, and He adds no sorrow with it."[254] I know this truth to be factual, and it is obvious throughout the Bible that God delights in blessing His children. But often when we go through a time of abundance there can be a twinge of guilt as to why we are blessed while another is hurting. Surely it's not because we are more faithful or diligent than others. There is definitely no merit on our part to deserve the blessings of God's grace. And in God's providence, He has compassion and mercy upon whomever He chooses to bless.[255] Paul the Apostle had to learn this truth as well:

> "For I have learned in whatever state I am, to be content; I know how to be abased, and I know how to abound. Everywhere and in all things I have learned both to be full and to be hungry, both to abound and to suffer need. I can do all things through Christ who strengthens me."[256]

It is through Christ's strength that we can endure suffering, and it is through His love and kindness that we can gain perspective of His gracious bounty. Whether in blessing or hardship, the *whys* of life astound us.

---

254 Proverbs 10:22 (NKJV).

255 Romans 9:14-24.

256 Philippians 4:11-13 (NKJV).

As I reflect on the incongruence of blessings and hardships I come to the conclusion, "but God!" So much of life comes to the finale of this repeated exclamation, "but God." God is silent throughout the weeks of discourse between Job and his friends as they share their conflicting views of "why." Finally, in Chapters 38-42, God speaks for Himself. Ultimately, God gives no excuses or vindications, but simply declares that He is God. We all deserved wrath, "*But God*, who is rich in mercy, because of His great love with which He loved us, even when we were dead in trespasses, made us alive together with Christ (by grace you have been saved), and raised us up together, and made us sit together in the heavenly places in Christ Jesus."[257] Likewise, David butted in, saying, "Lord, I cry out to You; make haste to me! Give ear to my voice when I cry out to you … but my eyes are upon You, O God the Lord; in You I take refuge."[258] "Many are they who rise up against me. Many are they who say of me, 'There is no help for him in God.' But You, O Lord, are a shield for me."[259] Psalm 42 and 43 repeat the cry, "Why are you cast down, O my soul?"[260] And then follows David's exalting conclusion, "Hope in God!"[261]

Just as we don't worship God *for* the pain, we don't worship Him *for* the prosperity either.

When I sense the need to cry out and inquire into the mystery of God's ways and ask *why*, I hear "but God,"

257 Ephesians 2:4-6 (NKJV). Italics mine.

258 Psalm 141:1-2, 8 (NKJV).

259 Psalm 3:1-3 (NKJV).

260 Psalm 42:5, 9, 11, 43:2, 5 (NKJV).

261 Psalm 42:11, 43:5 (NKJV).

echoing in the chambers of my heart and I feel compelled to worship. Whether in a time of trial or triumph, the proper response to all of life's mysterious antinomies is this: to worship and to hope in the Lord. When Job got the news that he had lost all of his loved ones, "he fell to the ground and worshiped."[262] When God delivered the Israelites from the bondage of Egypt, they worshiped.[263] When David received the promised blessing of God upon his life and posterity, he worshiped.[264] In fact, when human history culminates in Revelation, we will all worship in harmony with the heavenly beings forever and ever as God fulfills His love upon us in its ultimate expression.[265]

> "Now I, John, saw and heard these things. And when I heard and saw, I fell down to worship before the feet of the angel who showed me these things. Then he said to me, 'See that you do not do that. For I am your fellow servant and of your brethren the prophets, and of those who keep the words of this Book. Worship God.'"[266]

According to the Scriptures, the entirety of human history begins and ends with worship.[267]

We would do well to learn, as Paul had to learn, whether in great pain or great prosperity, *worship God.* And just as

262 Job 1:20 (NKJV).
263 Exodus 15.
264 2 Samuel 7:18-29.
265 Revelation 5:8-14; 7:11-12; 11:15-18.
266 Revelation 22:9 (NKJV).
267 See Job 38:4-7 and Revelation 22.

we don't worship God *for* the pain, we don't worship Him *for* the prosperity either. We worship God because He is God. We worship Him in our pain and in our prosperity because He first loved us. Now of course, we perhaps tend to want to embrace the pleasure more than the discomfort, but each experience has its distinctive testing and its unique fruit. It is my prayer that in whatever state you are in, that you would learn the contentment and joy of the "but God" worship.

One of my most amazing memories as a child was when my family was sailing to Catalina Island for an extended weekend getaway. It was a moonless Friday night where the sky was lit up with innumerable stars. I was alone on the bow of our boat looking at the reflection of the stars in the ocean and was mesmerized. It was a warm summer evening with the splashes of water aglow with bioluminescence from a red tide. Off the aft of the *Maramel* was a trail of luminous green in our wake as the plankton shimmered with green light when disturbed. And as if that wasn't glorious enough, all of a sudden a pod of porpoises came to play with us. Taking turns, one after another, these magnificent creatures jumped out of the water, surfing the waves at our bow. Their trails were lit up with intertwining streams of phosphorescent green that lit up the side of our boat. I reached over the port side trying to touch them as they launched out of the water and spouted one after another. At one point I noticed what seemed to be a parent-porpoise with its calf (i.e. baby porpoise), side-by-side, whirling and breaching. Together they seemed to be so playful and yet purposeful. I imagined that the mother was teaching her young about boats and how to bodysurf the wakes. I was so close that I could see the calf keeping its eye on the mother as it was led through the twists and turns and the ups and downs of their journey.

I cherish that memory as one of life's lessons in keeping my eyes on Jesus Christ at all times. I am reminded of the wisdom of Psalm 32, "I will instruct you and teach you in the way you should go; I will guide you with My eye."[268] Life can be exhilarating, and at times flat-out weird. There are the seasons of fast-paced twists and turns and ups and downs, but we would do well to keep our eyes upon the Lord for His guidance and counsel. Rick Warren's best selling book, *The Purpose Driven Life*, reveals the pathway of our ultimate destiny by keeping an upward gaze on God and His centrality to all of life's purposes. (Perhaps I will write a sequel one day called the *Porpoise Driven Life*.) It is heavenward contemplation that transforms the mysteries of the absurd into purposeful worship. It is such sensitivity to God's Spirit that even His glance would prompt our hearts toward His directed resolve. This subtle nuance may be the inspiration of Isaiah's writing when God revealed:

God sometimes speaks with a whisper, and that is why we need to draw close to Him.

> "In returning and rest you shall be saved; in quietness and confidence shall be your strength... Therefore the LORD will wait, that He may be gracious to you;

268 Psalm 32:8 (NKJV).

> and therefore He will be exalted, that He may have mercy on you. For the LORD is a God of justice; blessed are all those who wait for Him.... your ears shall hear a word behind you, saying, 'This is the way, walk in it,' whenever you turn to the right hand or whenever you turn to the left."[269]

I have learned that God sometimes speaks with a whisper, and that is why we need to draw close to Him. Such was the case for Elijah when he was alone in a cave, depressed and hiding from his adversary, Jezebel. It was in this place of solitude that God spoke to Elijah in a still, small voice.[270] Whether it's a whisper or a glance, the Lord is intimately present to guide us through the darkest seasons of life when even the faintest of lights is enough to see His straight and narrow path.

When Jesus called two of His early disciples, He simply said, "Come and see."[271] Much of the learning that took place among Jesus' followers was simply watching, listening, and eventually doing as He had done. Years later, it was the Apostle John, who wrote of the intimate relationship the disciples had with Jesus,

> "That which was from the beginning, which we have heard, which we have seen with our eyes, which we looked upon and have touched with our

269 Isaiah 30:15, 18, 21 (NKJV).

270 Then He said, "Go out, and stand on the mountain before the LORD." And behold, the LORD passed by, and a great and strong wind tore into the mountains and broke the rocks in pieces before the LORD, *but* the LORD *was* not in the wind; and after the wind an earthquake, *but* the LORD *was* not in the earthquake; [12] and after the earthquake a fire, *but* the LORD *was* not in the fire; and after the fire a still small voice." (1 Kings 19:11-12 NKJV)

271 John 1:39 (NKJV).

> hands, concerning the word of life—the life was made manifest, and we have seen it, and testify to it and proclaim to you the eternal life, which was with the Father and was made manifest to us—that which we have seen and heard we proclaim also to you, so that you too may have fellowship with us; and indeed our fellowship is with the Father and with his Son Jesus Christ."[272]

Though they were witness to the wonderful presence, teachings, and miracles of Jesus, even the disciples at times seemed to get distracted by their circumstances to lower their gaze from the Christ. Jesus chided Philip for wanting to see the Father after having spent over three years with Jesus: "Don't you know Me, Philip, even after I have been among you such a long time? Anyone who has seen Me has seen the Father. How can you say, 'Show us the Father'?"[273] It was the glance from the rejected Christ that was sufficient enough to bring deep conviction and tears to Peter upon the crowing of a rooster.[274]

There are many subtle ways that God leads His people through perilous times. One of the most challenging is when God is intentionally silent to our pleas. There are those seasons when we may not even hear a hint of a whisper or have a sense of His glance; though He is nonetheless

---

272 1 John 1:1-3 (ESV).

273 John 14:9 (NIV).

274 "Then after about an hour had passed, another confidently affirmed, saying, 'Surely this *fellow* also was with Him, for he is a Galilean.' But Peter said, 'Man, I do not know what you are saying!' Immediately, while he was still speaking, the rooster crowed. And the Lord turned and looked at Peter. Then Peter remembered the word of the Lord, how He had said to him, 'Before the rooster crows, you will deny Me three times.' So Peter went out and wept bitterly." (Luke 22:59-62 NKJV).

purposeful. Such was the situation for the desperate Syro-Phoenician woman who came to Jesus begging for her daughter's release from a demon:

> "Then Jesus went out from there and departed to the region of Tyre and Sidon. And behold, a woman of Canaan came from that region and cried out to Him, saying, 'Have mercy on me, O Lord, Son of David! My daughter is severely demon-possessed.' But He answered her not a word. And His disciples came and urged Him, saying, 'Send her away, for she cries out after us.' But He answered and said, 'I was not sent except to the lost sheep of the house of Israel. Then she came and worshiped Him, saying, 'Lord, help me!' But He answered and said, 'It is not good to take the children's bread and throw *it* to the little dogs.' And she said, 'Yes, Lord, yet even the little dogs eat the crumbs which fall from their masters' table.' Then Jesus answered and said to her, 'O woman, great *is* your faith! Let it be to you as you desire.' And her daughter was healed from that very hour."[275]

There is little that is more heartwrenching than to hear the cries of a mother's anguish over the suffering of her child. And yet, Jesus "answered her not a word." His silence was followed by the apparent prejudiced inconvenience of the disciples. This was in turn followed by the

275 Matthew 15:21-28 (NKJV). See also, Mark 7:24-30.

Lord's statement that He wasn't sent for the Gentiles at this time, but for the Jews. However, rather than being embittered by the silence of the Son of David and by the harsh treatment of the disciples, this brokenhearted mother chose a response of worship. What was unknown to all who were present was that Jesus was confirming the promises to the nation of Israel that the Gentiles would have the gospel hope. Jesus was fulfilling the Old Testament prophecies that through the Jews, salvation would come to the Gentiles.[276] Once again, God's ways are much higher than our ways and His thoughts are above our thoughts. When the Lord appears to be silent to our prayers, this is when our faith must rest in the foundation that God is good and that we are not abandoned. We are assured throughout the Bible that God is with us, and that He is at work to fulfill His glorious and perfect plans, even if it doesn't make sense on this side of eternity.

As a pastor and chaplain, I have been privileged to preside at literally hundreds of memorial services to honor the lives of God's beloved people who have passed away. From God's point of view, "Precious in the sight of the LORD is the death of His saints."[277] From our vantage point, death can be inexplicable, mysterious, and strange. I am frequently reminded during these times that we are very limited in understanding the divine perspectives of God's majestic purposes. At these memorial services there are often beautiful flower arrangements as family and friends gather to celebrate a person's life. While speaking from

276 See Romans 15:7-13.

277 Psalm 116:15 (ESV).

the podium, I am often positioned behind these beautiful wreaths. It is there that I see a gnarled bunch of stems and twist-ties that were intentionally arranged by the florists. To the audience, the florists' artwork portrays a beautiful tribute of splendor. From the backside, the beauty is veiled. Such is the case on this side of heaven as our limited perspective occasionally sees the gnarly side of an eternal bouquet that resonates God's glorious handiwork in eternity. "For now we see in a mirror dimly, but then face to face. Now I know in part; then I shall know fully, even as I have been fully known. So now faith, hope, and love abide, these three; but the greatest of these is love."[278] When God is silent, trust and worship Him. When He speaks, trust and worship Him. When the twists and turns of life shake us to the core, *trust and worship him.* We need to keep our eyes on Jesus and trust that He is orchestrating a wondrous purpose that will one day make sense when we see Him face to face.

And by God's grace, this is a choice we can make on *porpoise.*

Holding on Tight: Things to Consider

<u>GROWING IN GRACE:</u> During very difficult times, Paul the Apostle sent encouragement to the church in Rome when he wrote: "Now may the God of hope fill you with all joy and peace in believing, that you may abound in hope by the power of the

278 1 Corinthians 13:12-13 (ESV).

Holy Spirit."[279] As we learn to trust in the Lord in every situation, our hope can become pervasive in any situation. Pick a couple of these verses to memorize this week as you write them down and carry them with you:

- "Trust in the LORD with all your heart, and lean not on your own understanding; in all your ways acknowledge Him, and He shall direct your paths."[280]
- "Be strong and courageous. Do not be afraid; do not be discouraged, for the LORD your God will be with you wherever you go."[281]
- "Those who know your name trust in you, for you, LORD, have never forsaken those who seek you."[282]
- "Behold, God is my salvation, I will trust and not be afraid; 'For YAH, the LORD, is my strength and song; He also has become my salvation."[283]
- "For I know the thoughts that I think toward you, says the LORD, thoughts of peace and not of evil, to give you a future and a hope. Then you will call upon Me and go and pray to Me, and I will listen to you. And you will seek Me and find Me, when you search for Me with all your heart."[284]

PRACTICAL CONSIDERATIONS: Earlier it was suggested that in the midst of overwhelming situations it is helpful to take

279 Romans 15:13 (NKJV).
280 Proverbs 3:5-6 (NKJV).
281 Joshua 1:9 (NIV).
282 Psalm 9:10 (NIV).
283 Isaiah 12:2 (NKJV).
284 Jeremiah 29:11-13 (NKJV).

time out for a period of respite and quiet. However, at other times we may need to deal with our pressures through activity. Consider the following items that may help you in experiencing a catharsis or ventilation of your stress arousal:

- Engage in physical exercise and recreation.
- Make time for enjoyable activities that enhance your wellbeing.
- Take a long walk at a location that possesses good memories.
- Keep busy. When sitting, enjoy the motion of a rocking chair.
- Play family games with friends and loved ones.
- Remember the four L's of vitality–live, love, laugh, and learn.
- Take time to journal. Keeping a journal helps process the trauma.
- Engage in activities, hobbies, and interests other than professional.
- Invest in opportunities that promote personal and interpersonal growth.

CHAPTER THIRTEEN

God is on the Throne

In any public agency, a number of significant management changes occur when the senior leader retires. Such has been the case for the San Diego Fire-Rescue Department. In my service for over twenty years as a fire chaplain it has been my privilege to serve under the leadership of five fire chiefs. Each leadership change has contributed new elements to the fire department's operations and culture. During one of these transitional changes, it was a blessing for the City of San Diego to enlist the service of Fire Chief Jeff Bowman who transitioned from the Anaheim Fire Department. (It was a suitable fit for Chief Bowman to come from Anaheim given that he would still have a chaplain named Mickey in San Diego.)

In his years of tutelage Jeff became a good friend of the legendary basketball coach, John Wooden of UCLA. From this mentoring relationship, Chief Bowman developed the essential priorities of the department's "Four F's" philosophy. The "Four F's" have become the foundation for a culture that focuses on developing and empowering respectable firefighters. The "Four F's" are: *faith, family, friends,* and *fire department.* Essential to this paradigm is the concept that if the SDFD personnel had the foundations of healthy faith, family, and friendships, the fire department will be equipped with well-adjusted public servants. This model of living is transferable to any facet of life or institution. How we order our lives around these basic fundamentals has many far-reaching impacts. And where these priorities have been neglected or misguided, one doesn't have to search too far to discover the negative effects in the lives of people and the organizations in which they serve.

However, what happens when these essentials are the very means by which we are traumatized? The domains of faith, family, and friends are supposed to be places of safety and refuge. But for many, these sacred places are the means by which people have been most severely violated. Our home and our place of worship should be communities of security, protection, and growth. Yet there are countless tales where these revered sanctuaries have become the means of horrific assaults. When the onslaught of abuse happens from those closest to us, the complexities of the resulting pain can become fertile soil for potential bitterness and hatred. Where do we turn when the sacred foundations have crumbled? To whom can we go for perspective and understanding? How can we overcome such surmounting obstacles to return to the realm of *normal?*

Can *normal* even be a reality? Some of the darkest and most horrific circumstances of life can challenge one's faith to question if certain situations can ever be redeemed on this side of eternity. Yet, when we rest in the fact that God is sovereign over the most tragic of losses, we are assured that all will be reconciled, even if the timing isn't until we are with Him in heaven.

One type of pain and suffering that has devastating effects on a person's identity and ability to function is sexual abuse. From a national telephone survey of male and female victims of prior sexual abuse, twenty-seven percent of women and sixteen percent of men reported victimization. Of this population, forty-two percent of the female victims and thirty-three percent of the male victims acknowledged that they had never disclosed this information to others.[285] As a result of this silence, this secret indignity can quietly inflict havoc in a person's life and relationships. Victims often bear this pain alone, with feelings of overwhelming guilt and shame, when in reality these injustices were not their fault. These wounds and scars go deep within the heart and psyche. The natural tendency is for people to hide and to cover up these memories, while some individuals altogether block these repressed memories from their consciousness. It should be noted that many abuse survivors are often highly competent individuals who are typically successful in their personal and professional lives, as they compensate for the adverse effects of an abusive childhood.

285 D. Finkelhor, Hotaling, G., Lewis, I.A., and Smith, C., Sexual abuse in a national survey of adult men and women: Prevalence, characteristics, and risk factors, *Child Abuse & Neglect*, 14 (1990), 19-28.

However, it is when subsequent trauma or stress is introduced that complications of related dysfunctions and challenges can occur.[286] Many find assistance from the support of a well-trained counselor where they can fully disclose their experiences in a safe, supportive, and professional environment. Many survivors of abuse have provided testimonies of triumph as they become *thrivers* over their victimization. Consistently, the thrivers affirm that they have been afforded an environment of safety and support where they have narrated their stories and have experienced the catharsis and mourning of their pain and loss. It is very important to seek out this safe environment where the story of abuse can be told and a survivor can receive supportive empathy, validation, and understanding. Survivors can be empowered through counseling and spiritual healing to resist the shame that is not theirs to bear. When an abuse victim understands that the hardship they endured was not their fault, they can experience a sense of release from the past, which is a genuine gift from God. In addition, thrivers are often empowered to reintegrate their history with new coping strategies and perspectives for ongoing growth and development. One of the best predictors for a positive prognosis in sexual abuse recovery is when the victim is assured that their account of the abuse is believed. Through counseling, there are opportunities for new options to be explored, and for the rebuilding of the ultimate foundation of a renewed and transformed faith.

286 See the following research articles for additional specifics on current research on the maladaptive impacts of abuse. www.ncbi.nlm.nih.gov/pmc/articles/PMC1446666 See also, http://pediatrics.aappublications.org/content/early/2014/04/09/peds.2013-2166.abstract

When we are able to clarify that the source of our pain is directly related to our perspectives on trauma, a new hope is made strong for our future. As these insights are realized within an authentic, empathetic community of faith, the power of God's presence can be widely experienced by many in need of this healing truth. Regardless of how or why these abuses have pervaded our lives and our society, be assured that despite the most horrific of traumatic experiences, God's power is very real. Ultimately, we are assured that all of our tears, pain, and sorrow will be swallowed up in the promise of everlasting life and pure inexhaustible joy.

Hope is not a mere religious optimism that endures life's hardships.

> "And I heard a loud voice from the throne saying, 'Look! God's dwelling place is now among the people, and he will dwell with them. They will be His people, and God Himself will be with them and be their God. He will wipe every tear from their eyes. There will be no more death or mourning or crying or pain, for the old order of things has passed away.' He who was seated on the throne said, 'I am making everything new!' Then he said, 'Write this down, for these words are trustworthy and true.'"[287]

Through the tempests that come our way, this heavenly perspective provides the hope that is set before us as an

287 Revelation 21:3-5 (NIV).

anchor for our soul.[288] This hope is not a mere religious optimism that endures life's hardships for some abstract, ethereal escape that possibly awaits us in the future. Rather, we have confident assurance since our hope is based on the fact of the resurrection of Jesus Christ from the dead. Jesus conquered death through the atoning work on the cross, and that guarantees the blessings "of the life that now is and of that which is to come."[289] As the Apostle Peter encouraged the early church in relation to their suffering, it was the victory through Christ's resurrection that provided the basis for hope:

> "Blessed be the God and Father of our Lord Jesus Christ, who according to His abundant mercy has begotten us again to a living hope through the resurrection of Jesus Christ from the dead, to an inheritance incorruptible and undefiled and that does not fade away, reserved in heaven for you, who are kept by the power of God through faith for salvation ready to be revealed in the last time. In this you greatly rejoice, though now for a little while, if need be, you have been grieved by various trials, that the genuineness of your faith, being much more precious than gold that perishes, though it is tested by fire, may be found to praise, honor, and glory at the revelation of Jesus Christ, whom having

288 "God wanted to make the unchanging nature of his purpose very clear to the heirs of what was promised, He confirmed it with an oath. God did this so that, by two unchangeable things in which it is impossible for God to lie, we who have fled to take hold of the hope set before us may be greatly encouraged. We have this hope as an anchor for the soul, firm and secure." (Hebrews 6:17-19 NIV) See also Colossians 1:3-8.

289 1 Timothy 4:8 (NKJV).

> not seen you love. Though now you do not see Him, yet believing, you rejoice with joy inexpressible and full of glory, receiving the end of your faith—the salvation of your souls."[290]

When your faith in God propels you beyond the pain of the moment, you will experience a depth of peace, joy, and love that surpasses all human reasoning. When life doesn't seem to make much sense, to know and trust that Jesus guarantees our blessed future—this assurance brings a refinement to our lives where faith is purified and our salvation is treasured. From this outlook we are encouraged to gain strength in the midst of suffering. Within the context of overwhelming suffering, Paul wrote,

> "Therefore, we do not lose heart. Even though our outward man is perishing, yet the inward man is being renewed day by day. For our light affliction, which is but for a moment, is working for us a far more exceeding and eternal weight of glory, while we do not look at the things which are seen, but at the things which are not seen. For the things which are seen are temporary, but the things which are not seen are eternal."[291]

The book of Hebrews shares this same encouragement, but from Christ's viewpoint. It was the eternal perspective

---

290 1 Peter 1:3-9 (ESV).

291 2 Corinthians 4:16-18 (NKJV).

and "the joy that was set before Him"[292] that Jesus displayed for us that becomes the security of our faith through suffering.

A number of years ago I was called upon to provide grief support to a beautiful family whose father and husband had suddenly passed away. By the time I arrived at the home, lots of extended family were providing care and were assisting in the practical needs of the moment. In time, the immediate family asked me to join them in the kitchen to discuss their options for a memorial service. As we sat at the dining table the kids shared numerous remembrances, reflections, and themes about their father's life. He was obviously a well-loved and respected Christian man. Many tears were interrupted by moments of laughter as they recalled both the sacred and the humorous memories. All of a sudden the youngest daughter, "daddy's girl," burst out with all the emotion that would be expected. She could no longer contain her anguish as she screamed, "Who will be there when I graduate from High School?! Who is going to walk me down the aisle when I get married?! Who will be there for the birth of my children?! Why won't my children have a grandfather?! I miss my daddy!" As you could imagine, the house immediately went silent as the home reverberated with the agony of a crushed heart. This young woman had reached a point where she could no longer contain the pain of her loss.

What do you say at a moment of extreme grief like this? At a loss for words, I simply bowed my head and

292 Hebrews 12:2 (NKJV).

quietly prayed for her and her family. I have learned that silence can be beneficial in times like this. During her verbal catharsis, her voice increased with intensity through each of her progressive challenges. Finally, during a pause her mother looked over at me and gasped, "You're the pastor, say something!" It was at that moment that I learned anew that silence isn't always golden during extreme pain. There was a cry for a response. There was need for perspective.

When foundations are being destroyed, God is still on the throne.

All were waiting upon my reply for some solace for her suffering. Breaking the silence, I spoke to this young woman what I believe God brought to my mind in an instant. I asked, "What would your father say to you right now?" There was a silent pause and then through the tears she said, "That's not fair!" Again I asked, "What would your father say to you right now?" To which she gently responded, "God is still on the throne." Unbeknownst to me, Psalm 11 was a family Psalm that this Christian father had always recited to his children during tough times. When the children came to their dad with their various trials and difficulties through the years, he would always remind them that God was on the throne.

> "In the LORD I take refuge; how can you say to my soul, 'Flee like a bird to your mountain, for behold, the wicked bend the bow; they have fitted their arrow to the string to shoot in the dark at the upright in heart; if the foundations are destroyed,

what can the righteous do?' The LORD is in his holy temple; the LORD's throne is in heaven."[293]

When we feel like the very foundations of our life are crumbling, our tendency is to want to run, hide, withdraw, scream—and a multitude of other normal reactions. Yet God reminds us that He has not left His sovereign place of control. When foundations are being destroyed, God is still on the throne. No matter what the present distress, God is present to be with us to deliver us, even when things don't make sense and our pain exceeds our reasoning.

Why was *God* allowing him to see all these evils and why was *God* not doing something about it?

Such was also the case for the prophet Habakkuk in the Old Testament. The nation of Judah was decaying in an era of political and moral collapse. As a witness to his country's pervasive evil and violence, Habakkuk cried out for God to intercede and bring justice during his nation's collapse:

> "The burden which the prophet Habakkuk saw. 'O LORD, how long shall I cry, and You will not hear? Even cry out to You, "Violence!" and You will not save. Why do You show me iniquity, and cause *me* to see trouble? For plundering and violence *are* before me; there is strife, and contention arises. Therefore the law is powerless, and justice never

293 Psalm 11:1-4 (ESV).

> goes forth. For the wicked surround the righteous; therefore perverse judgment proceeds.'"[294]

It was apparent that the foundations of the nation were being shattered, and as the prophet literally screamed for God to intervene, Habakkuk questioned God's silence regarding all of the injustices and wickedness he was witnessing. Why was *God* allowing him to see all these evils and why was *God* not doing something about it? For Habakkuk, the apparent insanity of it all intensified after he heard the Lord's reply:

> "Look among the nations and watch—Be utterly astounded! For I will work a work in your days which you would not believe, though it were told you. For indeed I am raising up the Chaldeans, a bitter and hasty nation which marches through the breadth of the earth, to possess dwelling places that are not theirs. They are terrible and dreadful."[295]

God's declaration defied the prophet's rational understanding of providence and the nature of reality. Habakkuk was shaken to the core of what he believed were the underpinnings of God's will and God's ways. God was going to bring justice to Judah, and yet His means were going to be through a very unlikely source. God would execute judgment upon the wickedness of His nation, but it would be through a nation that was even more wicked and violent

294 Habakkuk 1:1-4 (NKJV).

295 Habakkuk 1:5-7 (NKJV).

than Judah—the idolatrous Chaldeans. Through this divine exchange, eventually the Lord instructed Habakkuk in the ways of faith, "But the just shall live by his faith...the Lord is in His holy temple. Let all the earth keep silence before Him."[296] Once again, when the foundations of life and perspective are devastated, know this, God is still on the throne. It was a life lesson that Habakkuk eventually embraced with great confidence. At the end of his prophecy, he concluded that no matter how bad things could possibly end up, he would joyfully dance within the divine hope and trust in God's rule.

> "Though the cherry trees don't blossom
>   and the strawberries don't ripen,
> though the apples are worm-eaten
>   and the wheat fields stunted,
> though the sheep pens are sleepless
>   and the cattle barns empty,
> I'm singing joyful praise to GOD.
> I'm turning cartwheels of joy to my Savior God.
> Counting on GOD's Rule to prevail,
>   I take heart and gain strength."[297]

There is a profound, unexplainable strength and confidence that faith brings in the midst of a crisis when we are enabled to wait on the Lord.[298] I have found great encour-

---

296 Habakkuk 2:4, 20 (NKJV).

297 Habakkuk 3:17-19 (MSG).

298 "He gives power to the weak, and to those who have no might He increases strength. Even the youths shall faint and be weary, and the young men shall utterly fall, but those who wait on the Lord shall renew their strength; they shall mount up with wings like eagles, they shall run and not be weary, they shall walk and not faint." (Isaiah 40:29-31 NKJV).

agement when I seek for an eternal perspective when faced with the profound problems of the moment. Paul the Apostle's challenge to "set your mind on things above and not on things on the earth"[299] is a fruitful mindset for experiencing peace in the midst of a storm.

One of the most common experiences people face during a sudden calamity is what is referred to as Cortical Inhibition Crisis Syndrome. It is the occurrence of a dumbing-down of the brain when suddenly overcome with a hardship. Without getting technical, there is a physiological response in a crisis where the brain restricts the non-essential functions of our emotional response to a threat. People sometimes experience short-term amnesia, alexia (inability to read), agraphia (incapacity to write), dyscalculia (inability to perform simple math functions) or anomia (diminished capability to remember names—I have found that anomia also happens when you turn fifty years old, which is a shocking experience in and of itself.) I believe that cortical inhibition is one of those subtle gifts from God wherein we are spared further complications in our difficulties as life is stripped to the bare essentials. Once again, the rudiments of faith, family, and friends can become a safe haven where divine and familial love increases in an experience of support. It is during these seasons that the

Throughout the Scriptures, we are exhorted to recognize the brevity of life in relation to eternity.

299 Colossians 3:2 (NKJV). Also consider Isaiah's reassurance when he asserted, "You will keep him in perfect peace, whose mind is stayed on You because he trusts in You. Trust in the Lord forever, for in Yah, the Lord, is everlasting strength." (Isaiah 26:3-4 NKJV).

non-essentials, which normally clutter our priorities, can be readjusted for a healthier foundation.

When the fundamentals of the three "F's" are dysfunctional in their normal state, a crisis can further exasperate our pain. Family conflict, broken relationships, or a rejected faith are common reactions when one's foundations are somewhat fractured at the start. As can be expected, when a sudden loss comes crashing into a struggling marriage, a relationship can erupt with further escalation and eventual collapse. On the other hand, a troubled relationship can be shocked out of complacency through a traumatic incident, and instead be brought to a place of restoration. Hardship can actually move people to get the help that has always been needed. Due to the intense pain, people can be jolted out of their discordant status quo, as new bonds are created and relationships are enhanced. Once again, the upside of down can pave the way towards hope and renewal.

Recently I have been struck by just how many of life's memories seem to fade into oblivion. When we think back to our childhood years there are some distinct exceptional remembrances, but for the most part a majority of our history has been forgotten. Actually we only have to reach back a few years to realize that cortical inhibition is a natural part of the aging process beyond the normal crisis response experience. My wife and I revisited Northern Ireland where I have been privileged to train local firefighters in developing chaplaincy and peer support services. Over a span of three years, we were astounded by how our recall was distorted from our previous visit. Though the experience was very distinct, many of the details of our previous visit were lost and it was like seeing Belfast for the first time. Imagine what we would be able to recall in the span of eons.

I have come to believe that in the expanse of eternity most of our human experiences on earth will dissolve into a vague mist of a distant era gone by. In other words, when we've been there (in heaven) ten thousand years, bright shining as the sun, our earthly days will most likely be a faint glimpse of a brief memory. John Newton's *Amazing Grace* asserts this concept in relation to our failures and our desperate appreciation for grace. Throughout the Scriptures, we are exhorted to recognize the brevity of life in relation to eternity. James queried, "For what is your life? It is even a vapor that appears for a little time and then vanishes away."[300] Job declared, "Oh, remember that my life is a breath!"[301] Asaph reflected that our earthly existence is "a breath that passes away and does not come again."[302] David also understood this fact when he wrote, "Man is like a breath; his days are like a passing shadow."[303] With all of this as a foundation, Paul astutely understood human suffering in the context of the eternal reality:

> "The Spirit Himself bears witness with our spirit that we are children of God, and if children, then heirs—heirs of God and joint heirs with Christ, if indeed we suffer with Him, that we may also be glorified together. For I consider that the sufferings

300 James 4:14 (NKJV).
301 Job 7:7 (NKJV).
302 Psalm 78:39 (NKJV).
303 Psalm 144:4 (NKJV).

> of this present time are not worthy to be compared with the glory which shall be revealed in us."[304]

This in no way diminishes the very real agony of human suffering, but we need to realize that in relation to eternity, we will barely remember these moments, especially within the experience of our glorified existence. Throughout the Bible there are many testimonies of horrific suffering among the saints of God. And according to the witness of Hebrews chapter eleven, it was faith that carried them through, as they were awaiting the fulfillment of God's promises in the future.[305] We would be wise to take to heart Jesus' encouragement to let go of life's worries, anxieties, and fears as we seek God and His kingdom, remembering that God is on the throne, and that He knows our needs intimately:

> "And He said to His disciples, 'Therefore I tell you, do not be anxious about your life, what you will eat, nor about your body, what you will put on.
>
> For life is more than food, and the body more than clothing. Consider the ravens: they neither sow nor reap, they have neither storehouse nor barn, and yet God feeds them. Of how much more value are you than the birds! And which of you by

304 Romans 8:16-18 (NKJV).

305 "These all died in faith, not having received the promises, but having seen them afar off were assured of them, embraced them and confessed that they were strangers and pilgrims on the earth. For those who say such things declare plainly that they seek a homeland. And truly if they had called to mind that country from which they had come out, they would have had opportunity to return. But now they desire a better, that is, a heavenly country. Therefore God is not ashamed to be called their God, for He has prepared a city for them" (Hebrews 11:13-16 NKJV). Read also Hebrews 11:30-40.

being anxious can add a single hour to his span of life? If then you are not able to do as small a thing as that, why are you anxious about the rest?

Consider the lilies, how they grow: they neither toil nor spin, yet I tell you, even Solomon in all his glory was not arrayed like one of these. But if God so clothes the grass, which is alive in the field today, and tomorrow is thrown into the oven, how much more will he clothe you, O you of little faith! And do not seek what you are to eat and what you are to drink, nor be worried. For all the nations of the world seek after these things, and your Father knows that you need them. Instead, seek His kingdom, and these things will be added to you.

Fear not, little flock, for it is your Father's good pleasure to give you the kingdom. Sell your possessions, and give to the needy. Provide yourselves with moneybags that do not grow old, with a treasure in the heavens that does not fail, where no thief approaches and no moth destroys. For where your treasure is, there will your heart be also.'"[306]

Holding on Tight: Things to Consider

GROWING IN GRACE: Jesus offered great encouragement to His followers during times of distress. Whenever you experience

306 Luke 12:22-34 (ESV).

a season of doubt or despair, remember this encouragement from the Lord: "Let not your hearts be troubled. Believe in God; believe also in Me."[307] Just prior to Jesus paying the ultimate sacrifice for us to have peace with God, He gave a number of profound instructions. Take an extended break from your schedule this week and reflectively read through the Gospel of John, chapters 13-16. Let God's word wash your heart, mind, and soul as the Holy Spirit ministers to your current situations.

PRACTICAL CONSIDERATIONS: Do you occasionally find it difficult to fit everything into your schedule? We all have the same amount of time each day, but sometimes it is just a process of reorganizing the management of our time. Perhaps some of these suggestions below will assist you in better organizing your schedule:

- Establish your priorities and organize around them.
- Know your purpose and calling and avoid the distractions that get you off course. Learn to say "No."
- Create a daily "To Do" list and again prioritize as to what is most important each day.
- Distinguish between what is important from what is urgent and do the right thing.
- Delegate whenever possible to free up additional time.
- Plan flexible time into your schedule.
- Consider your personal energy capacity for your daily routines. Take care of your main priorities when you are at your peek performance.

307 John 14:1 (ESV).

- Keep a notepad available for thoughts and ideas that pop into your mind to write them down. This will help you in not getting distracted from your current responsibilities.
- Anticipate for problems and interruptions that can potentially crash into your schedule.
- Eliminate time wasters and identify projects with which you tend to procrastinate.
- Break down large tasks into smaller pieces and organize your schedule to accommodate multiple days to address them.
- Set deadlines for yourself and be disciplined to abide by them.
- Throw away anything you can, as this will eliminate tasks that you keep revisiting.

CHAPTER FOURTEEN

Why Do Wild Jews Eat Ear Fungus in China?

As a crisis responder, I have often heard the question: "Why would God allow this to happen to me?" This is an understandable cry from those who are experiencing an agonizing situation. As noted previously, there are many of life's mysteries where it is natural to ask, "Why?" and it is during these moments of anguish and distress that it is normal to yearn for answers. We are to be reminded that our challenges come to us through secondary causes, and that God is not the author of the evils of our pain. God loves His children and is always working to redeem and to reconcile the wickedness of this world, even when our circumstances press us beyond our comprehension. In our search for resolutions, sometimes the answer is beyond what we are able to grasp since we are finite beings in relation to God's eternal perspective.

Helping me understand the pervasive question of "why?" came to me in the form of an Asian culinary experience, of all things, when a missionary friend from China showed me a bag of *Wild Jews Ear Fungus.* Perhaps the question, "why?" becomes most appropriate when a westerner ponders the gourmet delight of those who eat *Wild Jews Ear Fungus.* So I ask, "Why do wild Jews eat ear fungus in China?" For sure, this is a fair question to be posed by someone from Southern California. Whether ear fungus is fried, baked, broiled, or boiled, it is beyond my grasp how it could become a delicacy in any country. I would love to see one of those American television cooking competitions throw ear fungus into the mix of required ingredients just to see the response of the audience.

Eternal truths of the infinite mind of God are flawless when viewed from His eternal perspective.

Different cultures have different dietary preferences. As is expected, the everyday cuisine of Asia is definitely distinct from the international foods of England, France, or Latin America. But even then, it's hard to fathom a culture that markets ear fungus. What's more, this product is actually a delicacy that is used to flavor soups and other palatable dishes. How are we to understand *Wild Jews Ear Fungus*? As you have probably already surmised by now, it's a translation problem. A better rendition of this product would probably be *Wild Israeli Mushrooms.* These special mushrooms, originally imported from Israel, happen to grow in the shape of an ear, hence, ear-shaped mushrooms.

Maybe this is a roundabout way to address this subject, but it works for me. How is it that God reveals in His Word that He is totally sovereign over all of our choices, while at the same time Scripture discloses our human freedoms? Within the finite human mind there would be an apparent contradiction. How could two truths both be accurate but appear to oppose each other? Theologians have another word to describe this apparent conflict—it is the word *concurrence.* Concurrence is "an aspect of God's providence whereby He cooperates with created things in every action, directing their distinctive properties to cause them to act as they do."[308] In a simplistic sense, concurrence is a description of how two opposing actions can take place at the same time, though they harmonize beyond our human reasoning.

A more modest understanding of this fact is that we have a *translation problem.* Eternal truths of the infinite mind of God are flawless when viewed from His eternal perspective. However, these realities don't always translate well in a finite, closed system. While I have great solace in concluding that God's ways are higher than our ways, and that His thoughts are higher than our thoughts, our extremely limited point of view makes it difficult to understand how things will translate within the fullness of God's plan. As Paul said, "For now we see in a mirror, dimly, but then face to face. Now I know in part, but then I shall know just as I also am known. And now abide faith,

308 Grudem, Wayne (1994). *An Introduction to Biblical Doctrine: Systematic Theology.* Zondervan, Inter-Varsity Press. Leicester, England, pg. 317.

hope, love, these three; but the greatest of these is love."[309] There waits a day in the future when we will know more completely how life's difficult situations were working for the glory of God. What we deem as horrific within our earthly experiences will one day be seen as purposeful and redeeming within the completeness of God's providence.

Joseph had this perspective after being sold by his brothers as a slave, being falsely accused of rape, being forgotten in prison, and then being lifted up as the second in command to the Pharaoh, leading to the deliverance of God's people. Joseph rightly instructed his brothers within the concurrence of God's sovereignty and his brothers' sinful choices, "But as for you, you meant evil against me; but God meant it for good, in order to bring it about as it is this day, to save many people alive."[310]

The Apostle John affirmed this concept as well when he encouraged the church of Ephesus, writing, "Beloved, now we are children of God; and it has not yet been revealed what we shall be, but we know that when He is revealed, we shall be like Him, for we shall see Him as He is. And everyone who has this hope in Him purifies himself, just as He is pure."[311] Someday God's family will see the eternal Savior face-to-face. We will know as we are known. At that moment, I believe all questions will be answered in the face-to-face reality of the presence of the Almighty God. When we see Him as He is, the infinite perspective will provide perfect clarity to all of our finite musings. What's

309 1 Corinthians 13:12-13 (NKJV).

310 Genesis 50:20 (NKJV).

311 1 John 3:2-3 (NKJV).

more, even the great shadow of suffering will be put into a proper perspective in the light of God's glory.

A number of years ago I was part of a team of pastors who were serving leaders at a pastors' conference in Mexico. For those of us who didn't speak Spanish, we were provided translators to assist us for our messages. A respected pastor friend, Bill Goodrich, was given the privilege of speaking at one of the main sessions. Prior to his teaching, he met with his translator to review the message details. Bill shared his outline and also made it a point that his interpreter understood a joke that he was planning to share for some levity during his talk. When the Mexican pastor heard the joke, he shared with my friend that American humor didn't always translate well between cultures, and that he recommended that Pastor Goodrich leave the joke out of his message. Bill contended that it was hilarious and would be funny in any culture. However, after much insistence, the interpreter won out and my friend conceded the point.

During his session, the local pastors were completely engaged with Pastor Goodrich's message and you could sense the group responding to the heart of what was being taught. Perhaps feeling inspired by the audience's enthusiasm, with a twinkle in his eye, Bill looked over at his translator and then segued into his joke. As my friend began to tell his humorous story, the interpreter suspended his word-for-word translation as he told the audience in Spanish that the speaker was now telling a joke that wouldn't translate well into Mexican humor. Bill then carried on with his funny narrative and then paused for the translation. His interpreter continued to explain that when the pastor got to his punch line he would tell the audience when to laugh, which in itself started to produce a lot of smiles on the faces of those present. Pastor Goodrich then reached the crescendo of his joke, at which point his interpreter told the congregation that this was the time to respond, resulting in a roar of laughter. Bill looked over at his translator and motioned that he felt his humor translated rather well. Of course later, Bill was given the full details of how the joke really transpired (the joke was on him), over which we all had a good laugh.

God is *always* working a glorious good through *all* of life's circumstances.

I have had my own misgivings when it comes to translations between languages. I once took my son and his friend on a surfing trip in Mexico and I was pleased to boast about a special spot I knew that had great waves. And sure enough, when we arrived, though the beach was crowded, we were the only ones to take advantage of the surf. My son was telling his friend how I knew all the good surfing spots as we enjoyed a solid couple of hours together in the water. As we exited the ocean, we came across a couple of signs that were posted on the beach which we had dismissed on the way into the water. The signs simply stated—*Peligro, Agua Contaminada*. Of course it wasn't until a bilingual beachgoer told us what the posted signs declared: *Danger, Polluted Water.* At that moment it became obvious that my prowess as an international surfing guide was completely negated by my ignorance of another culture's three simple words.

Over the years, I have heard of many other hilarious blunders that people have experienced when translations have been errant. I am certainly not asserting here that the eternal interpretations of our human suffering will be viewed as levity in our eternal state; however, I do affirm that God is *always* working a glorious good through *all* of life's circumstances. This fact completely transcends our finite limitation of what we often understand within our situations as being good, right, or just. The revelation of our eternal future affirms not only a greater meaning to our current grief and sorrow, but also the ultimate renewal of what is true and glorious:

> "And God will wipe away every tear from their eyes; there shall be no more death, nor sorrow, nor crying. There shall be no more pain, for the former things have passed away. Then He who sat on the throne said, 'Behold, I make all things new.' And He said to me, 'Write, for these words are true and faithful.'"[312]

And as such, there are no recorded questions in heaven that challenge God as to why He allowed things to be as they were. Instead, the echoes heard throughout heaven are the praises and worship of all creation declaring the glory of God and of the Lamb. All our questions will be dissolved in the wonder and amazement of our King of Kings and our Lord of Lords. Nothing else

312 Revelation 21:4-5 (NKJV).

will matter at that moment. All questions answered. All issues resolved.

> "Then I looked and I heard the voice of many angels around the throne, the living creatures, and the elders; and the number of them was ten thousand times ten thousand, and thousands of thousands, saying with a loud voice:
>
> 'Worthy is the Lamb who was slain
> to receive power and riches and wisdom, and strength
> and honor and glory and blessing!'
>
> And every creature which is in heaven and on the earth and under the earth and such as are in the sea, and all that are in them, I heard saying:
>
> 'Blessing and honor and glory and power
> be to Him who sits on the throne, and to the Lamb,
> forever and ever.'
>
> Then the four living creatures said, 'Amen!' And the twenty-four elders fell down and worshiped Him who lives forever and ever.
>
> After these things I looked, and behold, a great multitude which no one could number, of all nations, tribes, peoples, and tongues, standing before the throne and before the Lamb, clothed

> with white robes, with palm branches in their hands, and crying out with a loud voice, saying,
>
> > 'Salvation belongs to our God
> > who sits on the throne,
> > and to the Lamb!'
>
> And the angels stood around the throne and the elders and the four living creatures, and fell on their faces before the throne and worshiped God, saying:
>
> > 'Amen!
> > Blessing and glory
> > and wisdom, thanksgiving and honor
> > and power and might,
> > be to our God forever and ever.
> > Amen.'"[313]

It is certain that the future reality and grandeur within God's glorious presence will replace all of our *question marks* with *exclamation marks*. Life's tragedies may make it seem near insanity to even try to make sense of life itself. There are those seasons in life for us all where things just don't translate logically, no matter how we strive to understand. We would do well during those periods to take time to reflect beyond the limits of our reasoning, and to know for certain that God's promises are true. It is there that we

313 Revelation 5:11-14; 7:9-12 (NKJV).

will learn to wait upon God's heavenly translation through the lexicon of faith, holding fast to His truth:

> "And we know that all things work together for good to those who love God, to those who are the called according to His purpose.
>
> Yet in all these things we are more than conquerors through Him who loved us. For I am persuaded that neither death nor life, nor angels nor principalities nor powers, nor things present nor things to come, nor height nor depth, nor any other created thing, shall be able to separate us from the love of God which is in Christ Jesus our Lord."[314]

As a final thought, there are times when we may feel like the life we are experiencing is a huge mistake. It isn't so much the "why" of our situation as much as the "what" or "when" or "how" in which we want to ask for answers. As presented in the very beginning of this book, it is the "Who" that needs to provide the lens through which we discern all other questions.

There are times when our feelings can overwhelm us with guilt or even shame over the choices we have personally made that result in devastating circumstances. It isn't a question of God allowing something, but rather, it is a decision that we have initiated that has caused such hardship on others or ourselves. How do we sort through our

314 Romans 8:28; 37-39 (NKJV).

past faults when we are completely culpable for the consequential damage?

In filmmaking there is a concept with which I totally identify when dealing with my own struggles with failure. It is a common film editors' term known as a movie *goof*. A goof is a mistake made during film production that accidentally finds its way into the final, released picture. For example, a famous goof is seen in Brad Pitt's film, *Troy*, where there were a few frames in which an airplane can be seen flying overhead during a scene. The challenge, of course, was that the historical account of *Troy* takes place around 1250 B.C. In other films, occasionally minor set alterations or background items have been inadvertently changed between shoots within the same scene. Most go unnoticed until pointed out by an attentive eye. Once identified, the goof becomes an obvious flag of the editor's negligence.

In a similar way, our failures and the resulting misfortune tend to endure throughout one's life as freeze-frames that cause persistent anguish. Life's *goofs* can be quite humbling, and we desperately wish we could erase these glaring blemishes. We can forget so much of life's experiences over the years, but these significant failures freeze in our minds some of the most distinct times in our past that arouse a depth of emotional torment. Sadly, these freeze-frames within the film of our life narrative seem to linger as some of our most overpowering memories. However, once again we are encouraged in the Scriptures to hold fast to God's eternal veracity over and against our limited perspectives and feelings. In Christ, the result of our true repentance is that we are "a new creation; old things have passed away; behold, all things have become new."[315] David also embraced this freedom when he wrote:

> "For as high as the heavens are above the earth,
> so great is His love for those who fear Him;
> as far as the east is from the west,
> so far has He removed our transgressions from us.
> As a father has compassion on his children,
> so the LORD has compassion on those who fear
> Him."[316]

Just as we are to accept God's eternal providence in His engagements with our painful crises, so also we are to accept His eternal dealings with our sin and failure.

So, the next time you stumble through a painful failure or an exasperating situation that doesn't translate well for you in the present, pause for a minute, and meditate on your true hope in Jesus Christ and the future glory that awaits you. And as you ponder your translation problem, let a smile grow on your face, and consider picking up a bag of Wild Jews Ear Fungus. I hear they go great in a bowl of chicken soup. And chicken soup *is* always good for the soul, or so they say.

(And who are *they* anyway?)

315 2 Corinthians 5:17 (NKJV).

316 Psalm 103:11-13 (NIV).

Holding on Tight: Things to Consider

GROWING IN GRACE: While in the midst of challenging circumstances, it can be easy to lose perspective of how special we are to the Lord. If you ever find yourself questioning God's regard for you, reflect on the following verses:

- "Yes, I have loved you with an everlasting love; therefore with lovingkindness I have drawn you. Again I will build you, and you shall be rebuilt."[317]
- "Now therefore, if you will indeed obey My voice and keep My covenant, then you shall be a special treasure to Me above all people; for all the earth *is* Mine."[318]
- "For you *are* a holy people to the LORD your God; the LORD your God has chosen you to be a people for Himself, a special treasure above all the peoples on the face of the earth."[319]
- "You will be a crown of splendor in the LORD's hand, a royal diadem in the hand of your God."[320]
- "Then those who feared the LORD talked with each other, and the LORD listened and heard, a scroll of remembrance was written in His presence concerning those who feared the LORD and honored His name. 'On the day when I act,' says the LORD Almighty, 'they will be My treasured possession. I will spare them, just as a father has compassion and spares his son who serves him.'"[321]

---

317 Jeremiah 31:3-4 (NKJV).

318 Exodus 19:5 (NKJV).

319 Deuteronomy 7:6 (NKJV).

320 Isaiah 62:3 (NIV).

321 Malachi 3:16-17 (NIV).

PRACTICAL CONSIDERATIONS: In addition to all of the aforementioned suggestions for assistance in times of stress, the following coping strategies should be added to your list of options as supplements to eating Wild Jews Ear Fungus:

- Seek good nutrition, a balanced diet and engage in a regular exercise routine.
- Gain perspectives regarding your FUD factors (i.e. Fears, Uncertainties, and Doubts).
- Take breaks during the day and engage in helpful relaxation techniques. Embrace activities of leisure and simplicity.
- Avoid making serious life-altering decisions or changes during a season of duress.
- Strengthen your social support or accountability group.
- Advance your continuing education through personal study, reading, and classes.
- Know your own "triggers" and vulnerable areas of weakness.
- Avoid unrealistic expectations for recovery after a crisis. Consult a professional Biblical counselor.
- Understand your humanity and limitations and learn from past experiences.
- Develop realistic expectations about the stressors in your life related to family and work dynamics.
- Evaluate your own susceptibility to anxiety and worry in relation to your current life situations.
- Invest in positive time and experiences with loved ones.

Conclusion

On a recent Saturday morning I received three crisis calls from three close friends, all within a three-hour period. Each of my friends was independently shocked to receive dreadful news about a loved one. The first message was a husband requesting prayer for his family as they just received information that his wife's sister was killed in a murder-suicide assault. Her estranged husband shot his wife and then himself in front of their two young children. Shortly thereafter, I got the call from a co-worker regarding her brother being run over earlier that morning in a hit-and-run incident. My heart was overwhelmed with the suddenness of these two horrendous situations. And then within minutes, I received a text requesting prayer support as a family friend just received the news that her mother was diagnosed with stage-four cancer, which had already spread to the liver. In three hours, three calls, and three heartbreaks: three lives that were forever altered. It is bewildering that these three families woke up that sunny San Diego morning with expectations, most assuredly, much different than what came crashing into their worlds.

Studies reveal that close to eighty-three percent of the US population will be exposed to a traumatic event during their lifetime.[322] In 2012, there were 357 naturally triggered disasters registered. Research estimates that there are approximately 268 million victims affected by natural disasters each year.[323] That is a quarter of a *billion* people every year that are impacted by a significant crisis. As a consequence of sin entering into the world, pain and death have constantly marched around the globe at an appalling frequency. Though these statistics are distasteful and cruel, it is our faith in God that should ideally lift us above and through the hardships of this world. Biblically, we may know this fact with our mind, but practically, our heart can be challenged to live out this level of faith. And even the most faithful of believers sometimes stumble in the throes of terrible loss. Travail tests our pride and causes us to face the ultimate of quandaries. Within this context, I have learned that my life is not about me; in fact, it's not *my* life.

The Apostle Peter challenged the early church during an era of extreme suffering and persecution to hold fast to their faith and integrity, knowing that all wrongs will one day be made right:

322 Breslau, N. (2009). The epidemiology of trauma, PTSD, and other posttrauma disorders. *Trauma, Violence and Abuse: A Review Journal,* 10(3), 198-210.

323 Guha-Sapir, D., Hoyois, P., Below, R. (2013). *Annual Disaster Statistical Review 2012: The Numbers and Trends.* Brussels, Belgium: Centre for Research on the Epidemiology of Disasters, p.1.

> "But the day of the Lord will come as a thief in the night, in which the heavens will pass away with a great noise, and the elements will melt with fervent heat; both the earth and the works that are in it will be burned up. Therefore, since all these things will be dissolved, what manner of persons ought you to be in holy conduct and godliness, looking for and hastening the coming of the day of God, because of which the heavens will be dissolved, being on fire, and the elements will melt with fervent heat? Nevertheless we, according to His promise, look for new heavens and a new earth in which righteousness dwells."[324]

With assurance of this future reality, we are encouraged to keep our eyes on the eternal perspective and to live holy and Godly lives. In fact, Peter acknowledged that we shouldn't be surprised by some of our sufferings, as it is part of the believer's calling to share in Christ's suffering:

> "Beloved, do not think it strange concerning the fiery trial which is to try you, as though some strange thing happened to you; but rejoice to the extent that you partake of Christ's sufferings, that when His glory is revealed, you may also be glad with exceeding joy."[325]

It is this gaze into eternity that transforms a jaded existence into joyful significance and converts hurt into a

---

324 2 Peter 3:10-13 (NKJV).

325 1 Peter 4:12-13 (NKJV).

very real hope. I believe that David was clinging to this outlook when he wrote, "One thing have I desired of the Lord, that will I seek after; that I may dwell in the house of the Lord all the days of my life, to behold the beauty of the Lord, and to inquire in His temple."[326] Over a thousand years later, Mary of Bethany, the sister of Martha, absorbed this focus of desire as she sat at Jesus' feet, losing herself in His words.[327] Though her sister was busy serving, Mary chose that better perspective.

The God-centered viewpoint is where wisdom is birthed—in the academy of suffering.

It is this intimacy with our Savior that dissolves the anguish of the past and the anxiety of the present, cultivating the assurance of a blessed future. And it is this solace that recalibrates present moments, saturating them with true inner peace. We are promised that in every crisis, Christ is ever present. The writer of Hebrews was most likely reflecting back upon the promises of God given through Moses during the last few days of Moses' life when the truth was proclaimed, "I will never leave you nor forsake you."[328] We are to be reminded that setbacks are not only a time for *instruction,* but also for *reconstruction.* And when we rest on this foundation, we are bathed in the peace that transcends logic and reason.

This Godward contemplation is at the core of the most sacred of healings. The God-centered viewpoint is where

---

326 Psalm 27:4

327 Luke 10:38-42.

328 Hebrews 13:5 (NKJV). See also Deuteronomy 31:6, 8.

wisdom is birthed—in the academy of suffering. The fear of the Lord causes prudence to gain potency.[329] Hardship forges the purifying work of humility where we learn that the universe doesn't revolve around us. Andrew Murray is supposed to have remarked,

> "Humility is perfect quietness of heart. It is to expect nothing, to wonder at nothing that is done to me, to feel nothing done against me. It is to be at rest when nobody praises me, and when I am blamed or despised. It is to have a blessed home in the Lord, where I can go in and shut the door, and kneel to my Father in secret, and am at peace as in a deep sea of calmness, when all around and above is trouble. The humble person is not one who thinks meanly of himself, he simply does not think of himself at all."[330]

I would go even further to say that true contrition discerns its preeminence in thinking thoughts of God and exalting His purposes above all other concerns. Affirming that all of life is about God and about His glory and not about our wellbeing and pleasure is the deathblow to our pride and control. Even the oneness that can be experienced within marriage is to be an awakening to the reality that the joys within this relationship is first to reveal God, and secondly to encourage our transformation.

---

329 See Psalm 111:10; Proverbs 1:7, 19:23.

330 Attributed to Andrew Murray in Wiersbe, Warren W. (1989). *Bible Exposition Commentary: Volume 2.* Cook Communications, Colorado Springs, CO. p. 73. A great work on this subject is the book: Murray, Andrew. (1982). *Humility.* Whitaker House, New Kensington, PA.

How is it that we can think to defy these truths when all of creation shouts of the glory of God?[331] It is in Christ that life becomes life. We find life in our death as we exhale the stench of our mortality in the grave of our self-life. "I have been crucified with Christ; it is no longer I who live, but Christ lives in me; and the life which I now live in the flesh I live by faith in the Son of God, who loved me and gave Himself for me."[332]

Since God is in control, I can let go of the reins of my self-protection as He peels away the layers of my emotional fig leaves that attempt to cover my inadequacies, fears, and insecurities. Sinful rationalization, justification, denial, projection, and blame are swallowed up in the assurance of my total acceptance by the One who sees all, knows all, and has purpose in it all. Writing to future pastors and seminarians, Tim Keller encouraged leaders to:

> "Expect to suffer. Through many tribulations we must enter the kingdom (Acts 14:22)—and the ministry. There are things you cannot know without suffering. God has special tutorials in tribulation for his shepherds. Do not begrudge the seminars of suffering. His aim is to make you, like Jesus, a sympathetic shepherd. It's scary."[333]

---

331 "You created everything, and it is for Your pleasure that they exist and were created" (Revelation 4:11 NLT). "For everything comes from God alone. Everything lives by His power, and everything is for His glory. To Him be glory evermore" (Romans 11:36 TLB). "The heavens are telling the glory of God; they are a marvelous display of his craftsmanship" (Psalm 19:1 TLB). See also Colossians 1:16

332 Galatians 2:20 (NKJV). Paul also affirmed, "For you died, and your life is now hidden with Christ in God. When Christ, who is your life, appears, then you also will appear with Him in glory" (Colossians 3:3-4 NIV).

333 Mathis, David and Parnell, Jonathan. (2014). *How to Stay Christian in Seminary.* Crossway Books: Wheaton, Illinois p. 13. Forward by John Piper.

I, too, have learned that it is often through much study, much prayer, and much pain that the Lord sculpts a faithful minister. Indeed, this can be scary.

In teaching us to pray, Jesus had a central focus for His followers to learn the submission of aligning their requests within the will of the Father. Jesus instructed, "In this manner, therefore, pray: our Father in heaven, hallowed be Your name. Your kingdom come. Your will be done on earth as it is in heaven."[334] We are to lay aside all of our desires and burdens, to seek that the Lord's will would be done above our own. Essentially, we are to let go of our control as we realize God reigns and rules above and through all of our choices and experiences. We are to pray with the perspective that life is about God's priorities more than our concerns. It is with this insight that God's kingdom authority will accomplish His heavenly plans in all of our life's circumstances. When it is our priority to surrender our assumptions, requests, and aspirations to the will of our Father, God's presence, purpose, and power are made preeminent in our prayers for His glorious will to be accomplished. And not only did Jesus teach this essential precept, He also exemplified it. When faced with unimaginable suffering, Jesus surrendered His heart to His Father as He prayed in the Garden of Gethsemane, "O My Father, if it is possible,

Affirming that all of life is about God and about His glory and not about our wellbeing and pleasure is the deathblow to our pride and control.

334 Matthew 6:9-10 (NKJV).

let this cup pass from Me; nevertheless, not as I will, but as You will." [335]

In contrast to the surrendered heart, it is perplexing to me that when people choose to live outside of the boundaries of God's will and wisdom that they sometimes plunge into bitter anger and blame towards God when a hardship occurs.[336] Much of our anguish is birthed from a lifestyle that reaps the painful consequences of disobedient living.

My father was one to firmly teach his kids about the consequences of our actions. As a police officer, he was strict in enforcing his edicts. I learned vicarious wisdom once when my two older brothers exceeded their limits through a day of bickering. My dad finally had enough of their squabbles and let them know that if they had any more arguments through the rest of the day, he would teach them a lesson they would never forget. Well, as you can imagine, youngsters often lack self-control and foresight, and firm justice ensued. As a result of another quarrel, my brothers were seated in the living room with the threatening assurance that my dad kept his promises. He once again reminded them that he had given them a fair warning and

Much of our anguish is birthed from a lifestyle that reaps the painful consequences of disobedient living.

335 Matthew 26:39 (NKJV).

336 During hardship and loss we should learn from God's commentary about Job after he had lost all of his family and possessions and responded by worshipping God. It is noted that the Lord affirmed that Job never blamed God. "At this, Job got up and tore his robe and shaved his head. Then he fell to the ground in worship and said: 'Naked I came from my mother's womb, and naked I will depart. The LORD gave and the LORD has taken away; may the name of the LORD be praised.' In all this, Job did not sin by charging God with wrongdoing" (Job 1:20-22 NIV). Also note the first actions of Adam and Eve after their disobedience to God when they each cast blame elsewhere, "Then the man said, 'The woman whom You gave to be with me, she gave me of the tree and I ate.' And the LORD God said to the woman, 'What is this you have done?' The woman said, 'The serpent deceived me, and I ate'" (Genesis 3:12-13 NKJV). In a sense, Adam is seen here blaming God and the woman for his predicament as a result of his choice to disobey God.

that they would remember this day's discipline for the rest of their lives. Tears welled up in their eyes, as they knew our father was a man of his word. After a brief moment of preparation, our dad returned to the room with a plate full of small rocks. He then proceeded to put the dish in front of my brothers, signaling the lesson would now begin. His edict was that my brothers were not allowed to leave the room until they had eaten every rock that was on that plate. At this point, my older siblings began to beg for forgiveness with promises of passivity for the rest of their lives. With arms folded and a stern look on his face, our dad's tone grew stronger as he ordered his sons to eat rocks.

With no other option in their minds but to obey or die, slowly, with quivering lips and shaking hands, they each took up some pebbles and placed them in their mouths. However, their tears turned into nervous smiles when they began to taste the sugary delight of candy rocks—something they had never seen before. When the smiles emerged, our dad decreed grace for the moment, with the promise that the next time they defied his warnings they would be crunching on real rocks. An honorable father's love will always seek to build virtue in his children, even though the consequence of bringing redemption is sometimes painful. And it is through God's grace that He transforms us with the eternal destiny in mind that He will one day completely renovate us in totality to reflect the image of His Son.

It is normal to want to distance oneself from discomfort. Pharmacology is robust in assisting people in their pain remedies with aspirin, ibuprofen, Aleve, Advil, Motrin,

Tylenol, Vicodin, Demerol, Vioxx, Celebrex, Ultram, Valium, codeine, and morphine, to name just a few. But God is not honored when we engage in self-punishment that seeks penance. And sometimes, people medicate their pain, suffering, and failure with the abuse of alcohol, prescribed marijuana, and street drugs to numb nerves and dilute discomfort. Tragically, the very things that people often do to mitigate their pain beyond what is proper become the very things that multiply their problems with further complications and heartbreak.

To experience faith in Jesus Christ in a manner that is sufficient enough to resolve any of life's challenges is to experience the essential foundation of ultimate hope. "My grace is sufficient for you"[337] should be the echo of God's promise in our hearts whenever we are faced with circumstances that potentially rock our world. God's love will truly reach to the depth of any and all despair if we sincerely seek Jesus and the purposes of His kingdom as our first priority.

While from the perspective of life's hardships it may be tempting to cry out, "God is *nowhere*!" rest in the assurance that you have not been abandoned. Take refuge in the confidence that his promises hold true. God is on the throne. And even in the most painful of times, He is present and intimately at work to bring us hope and comfort.

Where is God in the midst of your pain?

God is now here.

---

337 2 Corinthians 12:9 (NKJV).

Appendix[338]

Love one another

John 13:34-35 – "A new commandment I give to you, that you love one another; as I have loved you, that you also love one another. By this all will know that you are My disciples, if you have love for one another."

John 15:12-13, 17 – "This is My commandment, that you love one another as I have loved you. Greater love has no one than this, than to lay down one's life for his friends… These things I command you, that you love one another."

Romans 12:10, 13:8 – "Be kindly affectionate to one another with brotherly love, in honor giving preference to one another… Owe no one anything except to love one another, for he who loves another has fulfilled the law."

1 Thessalonians 3:12, 4:9 – "And may the Lord make you increase and abound in love to one another and to all, just as we do to you… But concerning brotherly love you have no need that I should write to you, for you yourselves are taught by God to love one another."

338 All of these Scriptures are quoted from the New King James Version.

1 Peter 1:22, 4:8 – "Since you have purified your souls in obeying the truth through the Spirit in sincere love of the brethren, love one another fervently with a pure heart… And above all things have fervent love for one another, for 'love will cover a multitude of sins.'"

1 John 3:11,16, 4:7 – "For this is the message that you heard from the beginning, that we should love one another… By this we know love, because He laid down His life for us. And we also ought to lay down our lives for the brethren… Beloved, let us love one another, for love is of God; and everyone who loves is born of God and knows God."

Serve one another

Galatians 5:13 – "For you, brethren, have been called to liberty; only do not use liberty as an opportunity for the flesh, but through love serve one another."

1 Peter 4:9-10 – "Be hospitable to one another without grumbling. As each one has received a gift, minister it to one another, as good stewards of the manifold grace of God."

Exhort and admonish one another

Romans 15:14 – "Now I myself am confident concerning you, my brethren, that you also are full of goodness, filled with all knowledge, able also to admonish one another."

Hebrews 3:13, 10:24-25 – "But exhort one another daily, while it is called 'Today,' lest any of you be hardened through the deceitfulness of sin… And let us consider one another in order to stir up love and good works, not forsaking the assembling of ourselves together, as is the manner of some, but exhorting one another, and so much the more as you see the Day approaching."

Take care of one another

Deuteronomy 15:7-8 – "If there is among you a poor man of your brethren, within any of the gates in your land which the LORD your God is giving you, you shall not harden your heart nor shut your hand from your poor brother, but you shall open your hand wide to him and willingly lend him sufficient for his need, whatever he needs."

Romans 12:5, 13 – "So we, being many, are one body in Christ, and individually members of one another… distributing to the needs of the saints, given to hospitality."

Ephesians 4:25 – "Therefore, putting away lying, 'Let each one of you speak truth with his neighbor,' for we are members of one another."

1 Peter 4:9-10 – "Be hospitable to one another without grumbling. As each one has received a gift, minister it to one another, as good stewards of the manifold grace of God."

Forgive one another

Ephesians 4:32 – "And be kind to one another, tenderhearted, forgiving one another, even as God in Christ forgave you."

Matthew 6:12 – "And forgive us our debts, as we forgive our debtors."

Matthew 18:21-22 – "Then Peter came to Him and said, 'Lord, how often shall my brother sin against me, and I forgive him? Up to seven times?' Jesus said to him, 'I do not say to you, up to seven times, but up to seventy times seven.'"

Colossians 3:13 – "Bearing with one another, and forgiving one another, if anyone has a complaint against another; even as Christ forgave you, so you also must do."

Be patient and kind to one another

Ephesians 4:2, 32 – "With all lowliness and gentleness, with longsuffering, bearing with one another in love… And be kind to one another, tenderhearted, forgiving one another, even as God in Christ forgave you."

Consider one another

Hebrews 10:24 – "And let us consider one another in order to stir up love and good works."

Pray for one another and confess to one another

Ephesians 6:18 – "Praying always with all prayer and supplication in the Spirit, being watchful to this end with all perseverance and supplication for all the saints."

James 5:16 – "Confess your trespasses to one another, and pray for one another, that you may be healed."

Bear one another's burdens

Romans 15:1 – "We then who are strong ought to bear with the scruples of the weak, and not to please ourselves. Let each of us please his neighbor for his good, leading to edification."

Be united with one another

Romans 12:15-16, 15:5-6 – "Rejoice with those who rejoice, and weep with those who weep. Be of the same mind toward one another. Do not set your mind on high things, but associate with the humble. Do not be wise in your own opinion… Now may the God of patience and comfort grant you to be like-minded toward one another, according to Christ Jesus, that you may with one mind and one mouth glorify the God and Father of our Lord Jesus Christ."

Have compassion and comfort for one another

1 Thessalonians 4:17-18, 5:11 – "And thus we shall always be with the Lord. Therefore comfort one another with these words… Therefore comfort each other and edify one another, just as you also are doing."

1 Peter 3:8 – "Finally, all of you be of one mind, having compassion for one another; love as brothers, be tenderhearted, be courteous."

Discipline one another

Matthew 18:15 – "Moreover if your brother sins against you, go and tell him his fault between you and him alone. If he hears you, you have gained your brother."

Galatians 6:1-2 – "Brethren, if a man is overtaken in any trespass, you who are spiritual restore such a one in a spirit of gentleness, considering yourself lest you also be tempted. Bear one another's burdens, and so fulfill the law of Christ."

2 Thessalonians 3:14-15 – "And if anyone does not obey our word in this epistle, note that person and do not keep company with him, that he may be ashamed. Yet do not count him as an enemy, but admonish him as a brother."

Teach one another

Colossians 3:16 – "Let the word of Christ dwell in you richly in all wisdom, teaching and admonishing one another in psalms and hymns and spiritual songs, singing with grace in your hearts to the Lord."

Submit to one another

Ephesians 5:19-21 – "Speaking to one another in psalms and hymns and spiritual songs, singing and making melody in your heart to the Lord, giving thanks always for all things to God the Father in the name of our Lord Jesus Christ, submitting to one another in the fear of God."

1 Peter 5:5 – "Likewise you younger people, submit yourselves to your elders. Yes, all of you be submissive to one another, and be clothed with humility, for 'God resists the proud, but gives grace to the humble.'"

Bibliography

Arts, Herwig and Rolfson, Helen (1993). *God, the Christian, and Human Suffering.*

Beckwith, Francis J. (2000) God knows? *Christian Research Journal,* Volume 22, Number 4. Christian Research Institute.

Beek, A. (1990). *Why? On Suffering, Guilt, And God.* Michigan: William B. Eerdmans Publishing Company.

Beker, J. Christiaan. (1994). *Suffering and Hope: The Biblical Vision and the Human Predicament.*

Black, H. (1966). *Good God! Cry or Credo!* Nashville: Parthenon Press.

Bonar, H. (1930). *Night of Weeping or, Words for the Suffering Family of God.* Chicago, IL, Moody Press.

Boyd, G.A. (2001). *Satan and the Problem of Evil: Constructing a Trinitarian Warfare Theodicy.* Downers Grove, Illinois: InterVarsity Press.

Brandt, Leslie. (1977). *Why did this happen to me?: God's answer to human suffering.*

Bridges, Jerry. (2006). *Is God Really in Control? Trusting God in a World of Hurt.*

Bryden, James. (1953). *God and Human Suffering.*

Buber, Martin. (1983). *The Heart Determines: Psalm 73; Theodicy in the Old Testament.* Pennsylvania, PA, Fortress Press.

Buttrick, G.A. (1966). *God Pain and Evil.* Nashville: Abingdon Press.

Caputo, Michael. (2013). *God and Catastrophes: When Catastrophes Hit Humanity, Where is God?*

Cooper, Burton Z. (1988). *Why, God?* Atlanta, GA: John Knox Press.

Crowley, Paul. (2005). *Unwanted Wisdom: Suffering, the Cross, and Hope.*

Davies, Brian. (2011). *Aquinas, Thomas on God and Evil.* Oxford Press, New York, NY.

Davis, Stephen T. (ed.). (1981). *Encountering Evil: Live Options in Theodicy.* Atlanta: John Knox Press.

Dowd, Sharyn Echols. (1988). *Prayer, Power, and the Problem of Suffering.* Atlanta: Scholars Press.

D'Souza, Dinesh. (2012). *Godforsaken: Bad Things Happen. Is there a God who cares? Yes. Here's proof.*

Duportal, Marguerite. (2005). *How to Make Sense of Suffering.*

Eareckson-Tada, Joni. (2010). *When God Weeps: Why Our Sufferings Matter to the Almighty*

Evan, H. (1959). *Mystery of Suffering.* Downers Grove, III: Inter Varsity Press.

Farley, W. (1990). *Tragic Vision and Divine Compassion.* Louisville: Westminister/John Knox Press.

Fretheim, T. (1984). *The Suffering God.* Philadelphia, PA: Fortress Press.

Geisler, N.L. (1978). *The Roots of Evil.* Grand Rapids: Zondervan.

Glenn, P.J. (1939). *Theodicy: A Class Manual in the Philosophy of Deity.* St. Louis, MO: B. Herder Book Co.

Graeser, Mark and Schoenheit. (1994). *Don't Blame God! A Biblical Answer to the Problem of Evil, Sin, and Suffering.*

Graham-Lotz, Anne and Moore, Beth. (2013). *Wounded by God's People: Discovering How God's Love Heals Our Hearts.*

Griffin, D.R. (1991). *Evil Revisited, Responses and Reconsiderations.* Albany: State University of New York Press.

Griffin, D.R. (1976). *God, Power; and Evil: A Process Theodicy.* Philadelphia: The Westminster Press.

Gwinn, Casey (2015). *Cheering for the Children: Creating Pathways to HOPE for Children Exposed to Trauma.* Tucson, AZ: Wheatmark Publishing.

Hagberg, Janet. (2013). *Who are you, God?: Suffering and intimacy with God.*

Hall, Douglas John. (1987). *God and Human Suffering.*

Hall, Douglas John. (2003). *The Cross in Our Context: Jesus and the Suffering World.*

Harrington, W. (1992). *The Tears of God: Our Benevolent Creator and Human Suffering.* Collegeville, Minnesota: The Liturgical Press.

Harris, E.E. (1977). *The Problem of Evil.* Milwaukee: Marquette University Publications.

Hauerwas, Stanley. (1994). *God, Medicine, and Suffering.*

Heath, T.R. (1969). *In the Face of Anguish.* New York: Sheed and Ward.

Hick, John. (2010). *Evil and the God of Love.*

Houge, Adam. (2014). *I Know That God Is Good But Why Am I Hurting So Much?*

Inbody, Tyron L. (1997). *The Transforming God: An Interpretation of Suffering and Evil.*

Jones, E.S. (1933). *Christ and Human Suffering.* New York, NY, Abingdon Press.

Keating, James F. and White, Thomas Joseph. (2009). *Divine Impassibility and the Mystery of Human Suffering.*

Keller, Timothy (2015). *Walking with God through Pain and Suffering.* Penguin Group, New York, N.Y.

Kushner, H.S. (1981). *When Bad Things Happen to Good People.* New York: Schocken Books.

Laurie, Greg. (2007). *Why, God?*

Leibniz, G.W. (1710). *Theodicy: Essays on the Goodness of God the Freedom of Man and the Origin of Evil. http://www.gutenberg.org/files/17147/17147-h/17147-h.htm*

Lewis, C.S. (1996). *Mere Christianity.* A Touchstone Book, Macmillan Inc.

Lewis, C.S. (1944). *The Problem of Pain.* New York: The MacMillan Company.

Lucado, Max. (2013). *You'll Get Through This: Hope and Help for Your Turbulent Times.*

MacIntosh, Mike. (1996). *Tender Touch of God: Turning Your Hurts into Hope.* Harvest House Publishers. Eugene, OR.

MacIntosh, Mike. (2002). *When Your World Falls Apart.* Victor Books Publishers. Wheaton, IL.

McPherson, Miles. (2013). *God in the Mirror: Discovering Who You Were Created to Be.* Baker Books: Grand Rapids, MI.

Milazzo, G.T. (1992). *The Protest and the Silence: Suffering, Death, and Biblical Theology.* Minneapolis: Fortress Press.

Morgan, Christopher W. and Peterson, Robert A. (2008). *Suffering and the Goodness of God (Theology in Community).*

Morris, Jonathan. (2009). *The Promise: God's Purpose and Plan for When Life Hurts.*

Morris, Robert Corin. (2005). *Suffering and the Courage of God: Exploring How Grace and Suffering Meet.*

Oates, Wayne Edward. (1959). *The Revelation of God in Human Suffering.*

Oden, T.C. (1986). *Crisis Ministries.* New York: Crossroad.

Oden, T.C. (1983). *Pastoral Theology.* San Francisco: Harper & Row, Publisher.

Peake, A.S. (1983). Job: the Problem of the Book; Theodicy in the Old Testament. Pennsylvania, PA, Fortress Press.

Petrik, J. (2000). *Evil Beyond Belief.*_Armonk, NY: M.E. Sharpe, Inc.

Piper, John and Taylor, Justin. (2006). *Suffering and the Sovereignty of God.*

Plantinga, A.C. (1974). *God, Freedom, and Evil.* Grand Rapids: Eerdmans.

Van der Poel, Cornelius. (1999). *Wholeness and Holiness: A Christian Response to Human Suffering.*

Proudfoot, M. (1964). *Suffering: A Christian Understanding.* Philadelphia, PA: The Westminster Press.

Robinson, H.W. (1939). *Suffering, Human and Divine.* New York: Macmillan.

Rodin, R.S. (1997). *Evil and Theodicy in the Theology of Karl Barth.* New York: Peter Lang Publishing, Inc.

Rowe, William L. (ed). (2001). *God and the Problem of Evil.* Oxford, England: Blackwell Publishers.

Ryan CP, Robin. (2011). *God and the Mystery of Human Suffering: A Theological Conversation across the Ages.*

Schilling, S.P. (1977). *God and Human Anguish.* Nashville, TN: Abingdon.

Sia, M.F. & Sia, S. (1994). *From Suffering to God: Exploring Our Images of God in the Light of Suffering.* New York: St. Martin's Press, Inc.

Sittser, Jerry. (1995, 2004). *A Grace Disguised: How the Soul Grows Through Loss.* Zondervan, Grand Rapids, MI.

Stackhouse, Jr., J.G. (1998). *Can God Be Trusted?: Faith and the Challenge of Evil.*_Oxford: Oxford University Press.

Strobel, Lee. (2000). *Case for Faith: A Journalist Investigates the Toughest Objections to Christianity.* Zondervan, Grand Rapids, MI.

Russell, Bob and Suggs, Rob. (2014). *Acts of God: Why Does God Allow So Much Pain?*

Swindoll, Charles R. (2001). *Why, God?*

Thomason, Bill. (1997). *God on Trial: The Book of Job and Human Suffering.*

Tvedten, Stephen. (2015). *Why Do Good People Suffer?: The Spiritual Cure for Human Suffering.*

Vieth, Richard F. (1988). *Holy Power Human Pain.* Bloomington, IN: Meyer-Stone Books.

Weatherhead, L.D. (1936). *Why Do Men Suffer?* New York, New York: Abingdon Press.

Webb, Dom Bruno. (2004). *Why Does God Permit Evil?*

Yancy, P. (1977). *Where Is God When It Hurts?* Grand Rapids: Zondervan.